Microsoft Office 2010 Explained

by

N. Kantaris
and
P.R.M. Oliver

Bernard Babani (publishing) Ltd
The Grampians
Shepherds Bush Road
London W6 7NF
England

www.babanibooks.com

Please Note

Although every care has been taken with the production of this book to ensure that any projects, designs, modifications and/or programs, etc., contained herewith, operate in a correct and safe manner and also that any components specified are normally available in Great Britain, the Publishers and Author(s) do not accept responsibility in any way for the failure (including fault in design) of any project, design, modification or program to work correctly or to cause damage to any equipment that it may be connected to or used in conjunction with, or in respect of any other damage or injury that may be so caused, nor do the Publishers accept responsibility in any way for the failure to obtain specified components.

Notice is also given that if equipment that is still under warranty is modified in any way or used or connected with home-built equipment then that warranty may be void.

© 2010 BERNARD BABANI (publishing) LTD

First Published - November 2010

British Library Cataloguing in Publication Data:

A catalogue record for this book is available from the British Library

ISBN 978 0 85934 719 8

Cover Design by Gregor Arthur

Printed and bound in Great Britain for Bernard Babani (publishing) Ltd

About this Book

Microsoft Office 2010 Explained has been written to help users to get to grips with the integrated components of this package, namely, the word processor *Word*, the *Excel* spreadsheet, the presentation graphics *PowerPoint*, the application that allows you to capture and organise notes you gathered on your PC *Microsoft OneNote* and the e-mail and desktop manager *Outlook* (redesigned and much improved in this version). The latter is only bundled with the *Home and Business Edition* of *Microsoft Office 2010* and those editions above it, although it can be integrated with all other editions if bought separately. All these components are specifically discussed within the *Windows* 7 environment.

Microsoft Office 2010 is an exciting new Office suite that will help with the new demands and challenges to individuals and business. It offers additional tools on previous versions of the package that use Web technology to provide enhanced single user or workgroup productivity and the ability to access and analyse important business data more efficiently. It also offers future user-requirements such as real-time collaboration, and the ability to easily connect to various social networks via the new People pane. Further, the old File menu is now replaced by a new full-window interface which is also implemented across all the Office applications. This new interface is used for accessing all of the options related to the running application and the currently displayed document.

This book introduces each application within the *Home and Business Edition* of *Microsoft Office 2010* by itself, with sufficient detail to get you working. No prior knowledge of these applications is assumed, but the aim is to present the package in the shortest and most effective way. Enjoy!

About the Authors

Noel Kantaris graduated in Electrical Engineering at Bristol University and after spending three years in the Electronics Industry in London, took up a Tutorship in Physics at the University of Queensland. Research interests in Ionospheric Physics, led to the degrees of M.E. in Electronics and Ph.D. in Physics. On return to the UK, he took up a Post-Doctoral Research Fellowship in Radio Physics at the University of Leicester, and then a lecturing position in Engineering at the Camborne School of Mines, Cornwall, (part of Exeter University), where he was also the CSM Computing Manager. At present he is IT Director of FFC Ltd.

Phil Oliver graduated in Mining Engineering at Camborne School of Mines and has specialised in most aspects of surface mining technology, with a particular emphasis on computer related techniques. He has worked in Guyana, Canada, several Middle Eastern and Central Asian countries, South Africa and the United Kingdom, on such diverse projects as: the planning and management of bauxite, iron, gold and coal mines; rock excavation contracting in the UK; international mining equipment sales and international mine consulting. He later took up a lecturing position at Camborne School of Mines (part of Exeter University) in Surface Mining and Management. He has now retired, to spend more time writing (www.philoliver.com).

Trademarks

Microsoft, **Windows**, **Windows XP**, **Windows Vista**, **Windows 7**, and **Microsoft Office 2010** are either registered trademarks or trademarks of Microsoft Corporation.

All other brand and product names used in the book are recognised as trademarks, or registered trademarks, of their respective companies.

Contents

1

Package Overview

Microsoft Office 2010 is an integrated collection of powerful, full-featured, programs with the same look and feel that work together as if they were a single program. Office 2010 was specifically designed to allow you to work with your information data, either by yourself or to share it with others, quickly and efficiently.

Microsoft Office 2010 comes in six editions, each with a different mixture of applications (for an explanation on what these applications can do, see overleaf):

Office 2010 Unique Editions Stand Alone & Volume Licensing	Word 2010	Excel 2010	PowerPoint 2010	OneNote 2010	Outlook	Publisher 2010	Access 2010		SharePoint WorkSp	Communicator	InfoPath
Stand Alone Licence											
Starter Edition	☺	☺									
Home and Student¹	☺	☺	☺	☺							
Home and Business	☺	☺	☺	☺	☺						
Professional	☺	☺	☺	☺	☺	☺	☺				
Volume Licensing											
Standard	☺	☺	☺	☺	☺	☺					
Professional Plus	☺	☺	☺	☺	☺	☺	☺		☺	☺	☺

¹ Can be installed on up to three PCs in a single home.

Microsoft Office 2010 applications have the following main functions:

Word

A Word processor that offers almost every imaginable feature, including background spelling and grammar checking, integrated drawing tools, basic picture editing within a document, Smart Tags and Task Panes.

Excel

An electronic spreadsheet that allows the creation of 3D super-spreadsheets by using multi-page workbooks which support 3D *drill-through* formulae, and includes a long list of 'goal-seeking', 'what-if?' analysis tools and an excellent set of database capabilities.

PowerPoint

A presentation graphics application that allows the creation of slide shows for training, sales, etc., and includes such facilities as object animation, speaker notes, and recorded voice-overs.

OneNote

An application that enables you to capture, organise and reuse notes you gathered on your computer. It stores all your notes in one place and gives you the freedom to work with them later on.

Outlook

An e-mail and Personal Information Manager (PIM) that provides a full set of multi-user, group-scheduling functions. The Professional version of Office includes the Business Contact Manager add-on * that connects small businesses to their customers through integrated e-mail marketing and to their business data through integration with other Office Suite applications. This is useful for recording notes and pictures against contact records.

Publisher *

An application that allows the design and creation of printed documents with the help of publication templates. It can auto-fit text to frame sizes, provide inter-frame text flow options, and auto-wrap text around irregular images.

Access *

A database management system (DBMS) that includes a full set of WYSIWYG design tools for database, forms, queries and reports, plus a full Visual Basic derived programming language for developing specific applications.

InfoPath *

Streamlines the process of gathering information by enabling teams and organisations to easily create and work with rich, dynamic forms.

SharePoint Workspace *

Formally 'Groove'.
A collaboration program that helps teams work together dynamically, even if team members work for different organisations, work remotely, or work offline.

Communicator *

A 'unified communications client' that helps with productivity by enabling communication with others in different locations or time zones, using a range of different communication options, including instant messaging (IM), voice, and video.

Note: The Starter edition has limited functionality in both Word and Excel applications.

---

* This book is based on the contents of *Office Home and Business* edition, so applications shown in the above list with an asterisk or the add-on to Outlook are not covered as they (apart from Access) require either SharePoint Online, SharePoint Workspace, or Communications Server.

Built-in Consistency

All Office 2010 applications have a built-in consistency which makes them easier to use. For example, all applications now (including Outlook) use a simplified Ribbon which makes it easier to find and use the full range of features that they provide. If you have not used the previous version of Office (2007) then you might find this somewhat daunting at first, but once you start using the new interface you will very rapidly get used to it. Below, we use Outlook to demonstrate the Ribbon as this is new to this application, but is also similar in functionality to the other applications that make up Office 2010.

The Ribbon

Traditional menus and toolbars in Outlook 2010 have been replaced by the Ribbon – a device that presents commands organised into a set of tabs, as shown in Fig.1.1. The Ribbon was first adopted in Word, Excel, PowerPoint and Access of the previous version of Office (2007).

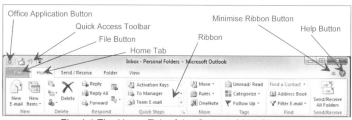

Fig. 1.1 The Home Tab of the Outlook 2010 Ribbon

The tabs on the Ribbon display the commands that are most relevant for each of the task areas in an Outlook Activity (in this case), as shown above for **Mail**.

Note the **Minimise the Ribbon** button which you click to gain more space on your screen. It then changes to the **Expand the Ribbon** button, which you click to display the Ribbon again.

There are four basic components to the Ribbon, as shown in Fig. 1.2 on the next page. These are:

Tabs   There are several basic tabs across the top, each representing an activity area.

Groups   Each tab has several groups that show related items together.

Commands A command is a button, a box to enter information, or a menu.

Quick Step Manager – Many groups have an arrow icon in the lower-right corner (pointed to below) to open an 'old style' dialogue box.

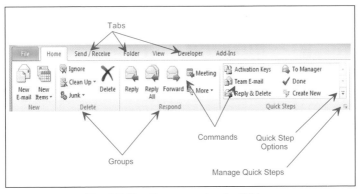

Fig. 1.2 The Components of a Ribbon

For each activity in all Office applications the Home tab contains all the things you use most often, such as creating **New Items** and **Deleting** commands and those used for responding to e-mail messages, meetings, etc., in the case of Outlook. If you were using Word, the Home tab would contain commands that allow you to **Cut** and **Paste** and those used for formatting text and for changing text font, size, bold, italic, and so on. Clicking a new tab opens a new series of groups, each with its relevant command buttons. This really works very well.

Contextual tabs also appear when they are needed so that you can very easily find and use the commands needed for the current operation.

Hardware and Software Requirements

If Microsoft Office 2010 is already installed on your computer, you can safely skip this and the next section of this chapter.

The <u>minimum</u> requirements for Office 2010 are:

- An IBM-compatible PC with a processor of at least 500 MHz, (1 GHz processor or higher for Outlook with Business Contact Manager), 256 MB of RAM (512 MB of RAM or higher is recommended for graphics features, Outlook Instant Search, Outlook with Business Contact Manager, Communicator, and certain advance functionality).

- 3 GB (gigabytes) of available hard disc space.

- Microsoft Windows 7, Vista with SP1 or XP with SP3.

- A CD-ROM or DVD drive.

- 1024x768 or higher resolution monitor.

- Connectivity to Microsoft Exchange Server is required for certain advanced functionality in Outlook 2010 and connectivity to Microsoft Windows Server running Microsoft Windows SharePoint Services is required for certain advanced collaboration functionality.

- To share data among multiple computers, the host computer must be running Windows Server 2003 R2 with MSXML 6.0, Windows Server 2008 or later.

- Microsoft Internet Explorer 8.0 or later, and Internet functionality requires access to the Internet.

- Grammar and contextual spelling in Word 2010 is not turned on unless the computer has 1 GB of RAM.

Additional requirements: Product functionality can vary based on the system configuration and operating system. Best results are obtained, according to our experience and if you want to run a few programs at the same time, with a PC running Windows 7 with at least 2 GB of RAM.

Installing Microsoft Office 2010

To Install Office on your computer's hard disc, place the distribution DVD in your CD/DVD drive and close it. The auto-start program on the disc should start the SETUP program automatically. If it doesn't, click the **Start** button, and in the **Search programs and Files** text box type **run** and

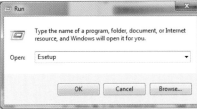

select the **Run** option from the displayed list. This opens the Run dialogue box, as shown in Fig. 1.3. Next, type in the opened Run box:

E:setup

Fig. 1.3 The Run Dialogue Box

In our case the CD/DVD was the E: drive; yours could be different. Clicking the **OK** button, starts the installation of Microsoft Office 2010.

With both methods, SETUP opens the Enter your Product Key window, shown in Fig. 1.4.

Fig. 1.4 Entering the Product Key

From now on you just follow the instructions given on screen, having made sure you enter the Product Key code correctly. Clicking the **Continue** button opens the next window for you to read and accept Microsoft's licence terms.

In the next window, you are asked whether you want to **Upgrade** or **Customise**. Selecting the first option, opens the Upgrade window with the Upgrade tab opened which allows you to select options between removing all previous versions of Office, keep all previous versions or remove only the core applications of a previous version, as shown in Fig. 1.5. .

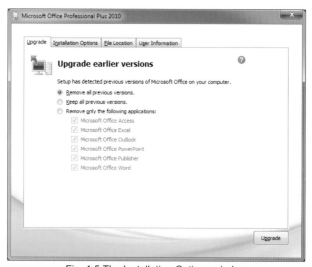

Fig. 1.5 The Installation Options window

The Installation Options tab, lists the Office 2010 applications to be installed and how they will run. This window is the same as the one you would have been presented had you selected **Customise** in the previous screen.

The File Location tab lets you set where on your hard disc(s) Office will be installed. The User Information tab lets you enter or change your name, initials and company.

We chose to **Remove all previous versions** and clicked the **Upgrade** button. You have to let SETUP do its own thing and not be impatient. At times the only indication that something is happening is the flicking light of the hard disc. In the next half hour or so, SETUP copies files to your computer's hard disc, sets up the applications and hopefully displays the Successful Installation window. A reboot is necessary to complete installation.

Starting an Office Application

To start an Office 2010 application in Windows, use the **Start**, **All Programs** command and select the **Microsoft Office** entry from the displayed menu, as shown in Fig. 1.6.

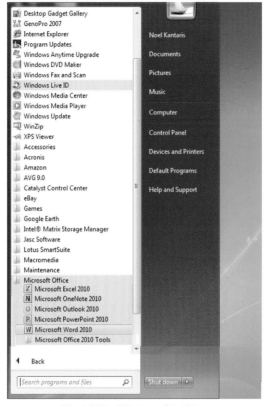

Fig. 1.6 The Windows Start Menu

Clicking on an Office application starts that application. Authentication of Office 2010 has already taken place (see bottom of Fig. 1.4). The installation and running of Office 2010 applications has been considerably simplified in this version of the package. If you were using the Outlook connector in your previous version of Office, you will be asked to allow an automatic update to it to take place.

The Mouse Pointers

In Microsoft Office applications, as with all other graphical based programs, using a mouse makes many operations both easier and more fun to carry out.

Office 2010 makes use of the mouse pointers available in Windows, some of the most common of which are illustrated below. When an Office application is initially started up the first you will see is the hourglass, which turns into an upward pointing hollow arrow once the individual application screen appears on your display. Other shapes depend on the type of work you are doing at the time.

The hourglass which displays when you are waiting while performing a function.

The arrow which appears when the pointer is placed over menus, scrolling bars, and buttons.

The I-beam which appears in normal text areas of the screen. For additional 'Click and Type' pointer shapes, specific to Office XP applications, see the table overleaf.

The 4-headed arrow which appears when you choose to move a table, a chart area, or a frame.

The double arrows which appear when over the border of a window, used to drag the side and alter the size of the window.

The Help hand which appears in the Help windows, and is used to access 'hypertext' type links.

Office 2010 applications, like other Windows packages, have additional mouse pointers which facilitate the execution of selected commands. Some of these are:

The vertical pointer which appears when pointing over a column in a table or worksheet and used to select the column.

The horizontal pointer which appears when pointing at a row in a table or worksheet and used to select the row.

The slanted arrow which appears when the pointer is placed in the selection bar area of text or a table.

The vertical split arrow which appears when pointing over the area separating two columns and used to size a column.

The horizontal split arrow which appears when pointing over the area separating two rows and used to size a row.

The cross which you drag to extend or fill a series.

The draw pointer which appears when you are drawing freehand.

Word 2010 also has the following Click and Type pointer shapes which appear as you move the I-beam pointer into a specific formatting zone; their shape indicating which formatting will apply when you double-click.

	Align left		Align right
	Centre		Left indent
	Left text wrap		Right text wrap

Fig. 1.7 The Click and Type Pointer Shapes in Word 2010

If you don't see the Click and Type pointer shapes in Word, check that the facility is turned on. You do this by clicking the new **File** Ribbon button to open the Backstage page of **Word**, click the **Options** button to open the Word Options screen, then click the **Advanced** option and select the **Enable click and type** check box. The Backstage page, which is common to all Office applications is discussed next.

The New File View

To see the new Office Backstage view, start Word 2010, open a file, and click the ▬▬ button. This replaces the old **File** menu across all the Office applications with a new full-screen interface for accessing all of the options relating to the application and the current document, as shown in Fig. 1.8.

Fig. 1.8 The New Backstage View

As you can see, many (in this case) Word settings that are not directly related to creating or managing Word documents, such as the **Save**, **Open**, **Print** and **Save & Send** commands, are now in the Microsoft Office Backstage view. From here you can manage your documents, protect your documents, prepare documents for sharing, and find other behind-the-scenes options such as user interface options and personalising your copy of Microsoft Office. These latter options can be accessed by clicking the **Options** button on the Backstage screen.

We leave it to you to explore the facilities available to you on the Backstage screen. It is worth spending some time here investigating the available options.

Getting Help in Office 2010

No matter how experienced you are, there will always be times when you need help to find out how to do something in the various Office applications. Office 2010 is a very large and powerful suite of programs with a multitude of features. There are several ways to get help, but don't look for the Office Assistant, as it has now been switched off for good.

The Built-in Microsoft Help System

To illustrate the built-in Help System we will use Word 2010 as an example – the other Office applications operate in exactly the same way. If you press the **F1** function key, or click the **Help** toolbar button shown here, the Help window will open as shown in Fig. 1.9.

Fig. 1.9 The Microsoft Office Help Window

The program expects you to be 'Online', or connected to the Internet. In fact, if you are not, it will attempt to connect you.

You can control where Help searches for its content as follows:

If you click the down arrow to the right of the **Search** button a drop-down menu opens as shown in Fig. 1.10. This has several online and PC based options. If you click the **Word Help** option under **Content from this computer** the Help system will only look on your computer for its help data.

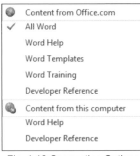

Fig. 1.10 Connection Options

Whether you are looking at Help online or offline is shown in the lower-right corner of the Help window, as shown in Fig. 1.9. Clicking this area with the mouse opens the **Connection Status** menu shown in Fig. 1.11.

As can be seen, this offers an easier way to tell Help where to look for its content. This setting is retained after you close the Help window, so if you don't want to search online you only have to set this once, whatever Office application you are working with.

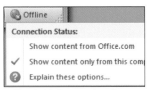

Fig. 1.11 Connection Status Menu

In the Help window the **Table of Contents** list opens up a list of available help topics in the form of closed books . Left-clicking one of these books opens it and displays a further list of topics with an icon, as shown in Fig. 1.12.

Clicking any of these opens the relevant Help page in the right-hand pane as shown in Fig 1.12 on the next page. We suggest you try looking up 'what's new' in every Office application you use – it is an excellent starting point in learning how to use the Office Help System.

Fig. 1.12 Using Word Help

If you want to know more about the options in a dialogue box, click the **Help** button  in the top right corner of the box. This will open the Help window usually with relevant help showing in the right-hand pane.

Searching Help

A quick way to find what you want in the Help system is to enter the text you want to search for in the **Type words to search for** box,

Fig. 1.13 Searching for a Topic

as shown here in Fig. 1.13. A search using 2 to 7 words returns the most accurate results. If you want to repeat a search, you click the down-arrow to the right of the **Type words to search for** list, and then click the search term that you want in the list.

The Help Toolbar

You can control the Help window with the buttons on the toolbar, as follows:

Back – Opens the last Help page viewed in the current session list.

Forward – Opens the previous Help page viewed in the current session list.

Stop – Stops loading a document.

Refresh – Reloads the current Help page.

Home – Opens the first (or Home) Help page for the open application.

Print – Opens the Print dialogue box to let you print all, or a selection, of the current Help topic.

Change Font Size – Opens a sub-menu to let you control the size of text in the Help window.

Hide/Show Table of Contents – A toggle key which closes or reopens the left pane of the Help window, giving more room for the Help text.

Keep On Top / Not On Top – A toggle key you can click to keep the Help window displaying on top of, or below, any open Office 2010 application.

We suggest you spend some time working your way through the Help system to find out how it works. Time spent now will be time saved later!

2

Microsoft Word 2010 Basics

Word 2010

Word 2010 is part of the Office 2010 package and is without doubt the best Windows word processor so far. As you would expect, it is fully integrated with all the other Office 2010 applications. You will find using Word 2010 to be even more intuitive and easier to use than earlier versions with additional functionality, particularly in the area of graphics.

The Ribbon, first introduced in Word 2007, which groups tools by task and commands you most frequently use, has been updated and consolidated. As with the previous version of Word, you get a live visual preview of the formatting in your document before you actually make a change.

What you will notice immediately as different in Word 2010, is the new Navigation pane displayed to the left of an opened document, which replaces the old Document Map from previous versions.

Chart and diagram features including three-dimensional shapes, transparency, drop shadows and other effects are also to be found in Word 2010, as are Quick Styles and Document Themes, which let you change the appearance of text, tables, and graphics throughout your document.

AutoCorrect and AutoFormat can when active, correct common spelling mistakes and format documents automatically, allowing Word 2010 to anticipate what you want to do and attempt to produce the correct result.

New to Word 2010 is the ability to edit images without having to use separate software for the purpose. Another image tool, gives you the ability to take a snapshot from a Web page and include it into your document.

Starting the Word Program

To start Word 2010, use the **Start**, **All Programs** command, select the **Microsoft Office** entry from the displayed menu, and click **Microsoft Word 2010**, as shown in Fig. 2.1.

Fig. 2.1 Using the Start Menu

You can also double-click on a Word document file in a Windows folder, in which case the document will be loaded into Word at the same time.

The Word Screen

When you start Word the program momentarily displays its opening screen, and then displays the first page of a new document, shown here in Fig. 2.2.

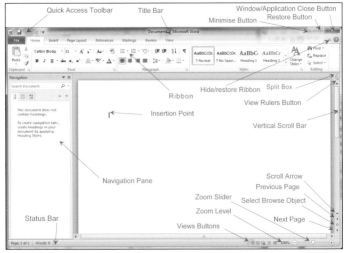

Fig. 2.2 Word 2010's New Document Window

Whether you have used a previous version of Word or not, the first time you use the program, it might be a good idea to refer to the Help System as discussed at the end of Chapter 1.

It is perhaps worth spending some time looking at the various parts that make up this screen. Word follows the usual Windows and Office 2010 conventions and if you are familiar with these you can skip some of this section, but even so, a few minutes might be well spent here.

Note that in Fig. 2.2, the Word window displays an empty document with the title 'Document1', and has a solid 'Title bar', indicating that it is the active application window. Although multiple windows can be displayed simultaneously, you can only enter data into the active window (which will always be displayed on top, unless you view them on a split screen). Title bars of non-active windows appear a lighter shade than that of the active one.

The Ribbon

When you first use Word 2010 the Ribbon is the first major change you will notice (unless you have used the 2007 Word version). The older menu bar and toolbars of version 2003, have been scrapped and replaced with the Ribbon. Please look at pages 4 and 5 for a general description of the main Ribbon components, including how you can minimise it.

In Word the Ribbon has seven tabs, each one with the most used controls grouped on it for the main program actions.

Fig. 2.3 The Home Tab of the Word 2010 Ribbon

A quick look at the Home tab, shown in Fig. 2.3, shows that it contains all the things you use most often, such as the cut and paste commands and those used for formatting both text, paragraphs and styles, such as changing text font, size, bold, italic and so on.

Clicking a new tab opens a new series of groups, each with its relevant command buttons. The content of the other tabs allow you to do the following:

- The Insert tab, displays groupings to enable you to immediately insert Pages, Tables, Illustrations, Links, Headers and Footers, Text, and Symbols.

- The Page Layout tab groups controls for you to set your Themes, Page Setup, Page Background, Paragraph and to Arrange graphic content.

- The References tab is used mostly with large documents and reports; to add and control a Table of Contents, Footnotes, Citations and Bibliography, Captions, an Index and a Table of Authorities.

- The Mailings tab groups all the actions involved in sending your personal and office correspondence. These include: Creating envelopes and labels, Starting a Mail Merge, Writing and Inserting Fields to control a mail merge, letting you Preview Results and then Finish a merge operation.

- The Review tab groups controls for Proofing your documents and to initiate and track document review and approval processes in an organisation for instance. It lets you handle Comments, document Tracking, any Changes made to a document and lets you Compare or Protect your documents.

- The View tab allows you to change what you see on the screen. You can choose between Document Views, Show or Hide screen features, Zoom to different magnifications, control document Windows and run and record Macros.

That is all the content of the fixed Tabs, but there are still others, as described at the bottom of page 5. Some Tabs only appear when they are actually needed. These contextual tabs contain tools that are only active when an object like a picture, chart or equation is selected in the document. These will be covered later as and when they crop up.

Quick Access Toolbar

The Quick Access Toolbar is the small area to the upper left

of the Ribbon, as shown in Fig. 2.2, and enlarged here. This is one of the most useful features of Office 2010. It contains buttons for the things that you use over and over every day, such as **Save**, **Undo** and **Repeat**, by default. The bar is always available, whatever you are doing in a program, and it is very easy to add buttons for your most used commands.

Clicking the **Customize Quick Access Toolbar** button ⊽ pointed to above shows a menu of suggested items for the toolbar. You can select the **More Commands** option In Fig. 2.4, to add others, or even easier, just right-click on a Ribbon control and select **Add to Quick Access Toolbar**.

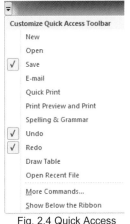

Fig. 2.4 Quick Access Options

Page & Object Selection

The buttons at the bottom right of the document area of Fig. 2.2, shown enlarged here, can be used to go to the **Previous Page**, to **Select Browse Object**, or go to the **Next Page**.

Clicking the **Select Browse Object** button, in the middle of the three, reveals a list of objects, as shown in Fig. 2.5, that you can use to browse your document. For

Fig. 2.5 Selecting Objects to Browse

example, you can browse by Page (going from one page to the next, by Section (going from one section to the next), or by Picture (going from one picture to the next), to mention but a few. To see which option is which, place the mouse pointer on an object and its function will replace the **Cancel** button.

The Status Bar

This is located at the bottom of the Word window and is used to display statistics about the active document.

Fig. 2.6 The Word 2010 Status Bar

When a document is being opened, the Status bar displays for a short time its name and length in terms of total number of characters. Once a document is opened, the Status bar displays the statistics of the document at the insertion point; here it is on Page 2.

You can control what appears on the Status Bar by right-clicking it and making selections in the Customize Status dialogue box that opens.

Fig. 2.7 The Customize Status Bar Screen

The Navigation Pane

The new Navigation pane is shown in Fig. 2.8 for an inventory of the contents of an imaginary flat. The headings that appear on the Navigation pane are of type **Heading1** as indicated in the Ribbon.

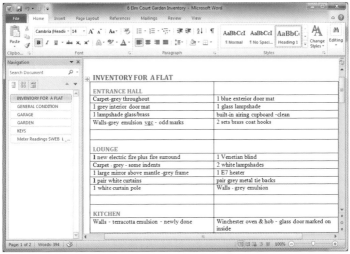

Fig. 2.8 The Navigation Pane Screen

The Navigation pane replaces the old Document Map of previous versions of the program. It displays on the left of the document and shows one of three views which can be selected via tabs at the top of the pane to do the following:

- allows you to browse your document by section headings which, as mentioned previously, only appear in the Navigation pane if they are of type **Heading1**. Such section headings are alive, meaning that you can drag them up and down to rearrange the document easily and quickly.

- allows you to browse your document by page, so that you can jump to the required page.

- allows you to browse your document by the results of your current search. This replaces the old Find dialogue box of previous Word versions.

When you type a word or a phrase in the Search box of the third Navigation tab, every match is highlighted in the document itself, and snippets from around each match appear in the Navigation pane, as shown in Fig. 2.9.

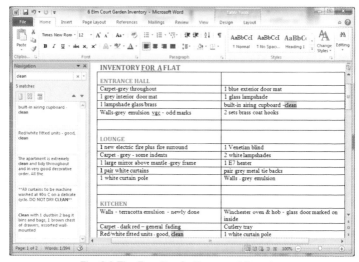

Fig. 2.9 The Results of a Document Search

Note also that since our document data was entered into a table, two new tabs appear on the Ribbon under **Table Tools**, namely those for changing the **Design** and the **Layout** of the table.

Creating Word Documents

When the program is first used, all Word's features default to those shown in Fig. 2.2. It is quite possible to use Word in this mode, without changing any main settings, but obviously it is possible to customise the package to your needs, as we shall see later.

If you are familiar with entering text in Word, or navigating around a document, you can easily skip the next few sections of this Chapter.

Entering Text

In order to illustrate some of Word's capabilities, you need to have a short text at hand. We suggest you type the memo below into a new document. At this stage, don't worry if the length of the lines below differ from those on your display.

As you type in text, any time you want to force a new line, or paragraph, just press the **Enter** key. While typing within a paragraph, Word sorts out line lengths automatically (known as 'word wrap'), without you having to press any keys to move to a new line.

MEMO TO PC USERS
Data Processing Computers
The microcomputers in the Data Processing room are a mixture of IBM compatible PCs with Pentium processors running at various speeds. Most have CD-ROM drives, while others are fitted with combo CD/DVD drives. The PCs are connected to various printers, including a couple of colour printers, via a network; the Laser printers giving best output.

Structuring of Hard Disc
The computer you are using will have at least a 300 GB capacity hard disc on which a number of software programs, including the latest version of Microsoft Windows and Microsoft Office, have been installed. To make life easier, the hard disc is partitioned so that data can be kept separate from programs. The disc partition that holds the data for the various applications running on the computer is highly structured, with each program having its own folder in which its own data can be held.

Finding Data Folders
In Windows you can navigate to your data folders in two different ways:
Method 1. Use the Computer entry from the Start menu and navigate to the appropriate folder holding your data.
Method 2. Use the Windows Explorer from the Start, All Programs, Accessories sub-menu.

Fig. 2.10 A Short Memo to Illustrate Some of Word's Capabilities

Moving Around a Document

You can move the cursor around a document with the normal direction keys, and with the key combinations listed below.

To move	*Press*
Left one character	←
Right one character	→
Up one line	↑
Down one line	↓
Left one word	Ctrl+←
Right one word	Ctrl+→
To beginning of line	Home
To end of line	End
To paragraph beginning	Ctrl+↑
To paragraph end	Ctrl+↓
Up one screen	PgUp
Down one screen	PgDn
To top of previous page	Ctrl+PgUp
To top of next page	Ctrl+PgDn
To beginning of file	Ctrl+Home
To end of file	Ctrl+End

To move to a specified page in a multi-page document, use the second tab of the Navigation pane, the **Previous Page** and **Next Page** buttons, shown in Fig. 2.2, or use the **Ctrl+G** keyboard shortcut. The latter can also be actioned from the **Editing** group on the Home tab. Both of these open the window shown in Fig. 2.11.

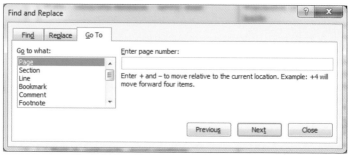

Fig. 2.11 The Find and Replace Dialogue Box

Styles, Templates and Themes

Fig. 2.12 The Styles
Gallery on the Home Tab

When you start Word it opens with a new empty document, and defaults to the 'Normal' style in the Styles gallery as shown in Fig. 2.12. This means that any text you enter is shown in the Normal style which is one of the styles available in the NORMAL template. Every document produced by Word has to use a template, and NORMAL is the default. A template is a special "starter" document type. When you open a template, a new document opens with the content, layout, formatting, styles and the theme from that template.

To change the style of a paragraph, place the cursor in the paragraph in question, the title line in our example, then move the pointer through the options in the Style gallery – you might need to click the **More** button to display additional styles. Each one is instantly previewed in the main body of the document, as shown in Fig. 2.13.

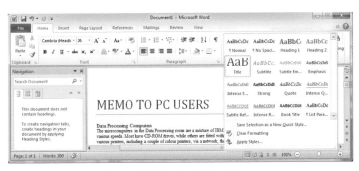

Fig. 2.13 Using the Styles Gallery

We clicked on the **Title** style to select it and the paragraph reformatted to Cambria typeface of point size 26 with a line across the page. Very clever.

Another way of setting a style is from the floating Style Task Pane which is opened by clicking the Dialogue Box Launcher on the **Styles** group of the **Home** tab, as pointed to here in Fig. 2.14.

Now with the cursor in the second line of text, we selected **Heading1** which reformatted the line of text to Cambria 14 in blue. We repeated this with the "Structuring of Hard Disc" and "Finding Data Folders" headings. Your memo should now look presentable, and be similar to Fig. 2.15 below.

Fig. 2.14 The Styles Task Pane

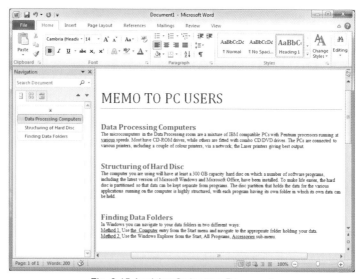

Fig. 2.15 Applying Styles to a Document

Themes

Fig. 2.16 The Themes Group

Every document created in Office 2010 is based on a Theme which can be accessed from the Page Layout tab of the Ribbon. Themes provide colours, fonts or effects that apply to all parts of the document, which simplifies the process of creating matching documents across all the Office 2010 programs.

Try resting your pointer over a thumbnail in the Themes gallery, and notice how your document changes.

Document Screen Views

Word 2010 provides five main display views, as shown in Fig. 2.17 in the **View** tab of the Ribbon.

Fig. 2.17 The Document Views

You can also view your documents in a whole range of screen enlargements with the **Zoom** controls from the Status bar. When a document is displayed you can switch freely between them. When first loaded, the screen displays in the default **Print Layout** view.

The main view options have the following effects:

Print Layout – Provides a WYSIWYG (what you see is what you get) view of a document. The text displays in the typefaces and point sizes and with the selected attributes. This is the default working view and all features appear on the screen as they will in the final printout.

Full Screen Reading – Provides an easy to read and very customisable view of a document. You can change the text size, edit the document, carry out commenting and reviews and see how the pages will print. Also in this view you have easy access to research, translation and highlighting tools.

Web Layout – A view that optimises the layout of a document to make online reading easier. Use this layout view when you are creating a Web page or a document that is viewed on the screen. In Web layout view, you can see backgrounds, text is wrapped to fit the window, and graphics are positioned just as they are in a Web browser.

Outline – Provides a collapsible view of a document, which enables you to see its organisation at a glance. You can display all the text in a file, or just the text that uses the paragraph styles you specify.

Draft – A view that simplifies the layout of the page so that you can type, edit and format text quickly. In draft view, page boundaries, headers and footers, backgrounds, drawing objects and pictures that do not have the '**In line with text**' wrapping style do not appear.

Changing Word's Default Options

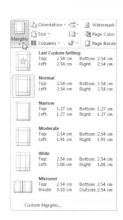

Modifying Margins

It is easy to change the standard page margins for your entire document from the cursor position onward, or for selected text.

Click the **Page Layout**, **Page Setup**, **Margins** button on the Ribbon, as shown in Fig. 2.18. There is a gallery of five pre-set options to select from.

Fig. 2.18 Changing Margin Settings

Alternatively, you can click the **Custom Margins** option to open the Page Setup dialogue box shown in Fig. 2.19.

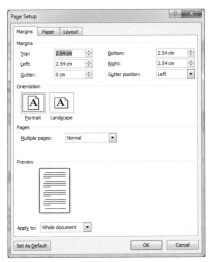

Fig. 2.19 The Margins Tab Sheet of the Page Setup Box

On the Margins tab of this box you can change any of the margin or gutter settings. The **Preview** diagram at the bottom of the box shows how your changes will look on a real page. The orientation of the printed page is normally **Portrait** where text prints across the page width, but you can change this to **Landscape** which prints across the page length, if you prefer.

To make the new settings 'permanent', press the **Set As Default** button and confirm that you wish this change to affect all new documents based on the Normal template.

Changing Paper Settings

To change the default paper settings from those set during installation, open the Page Setup box, but click the Paper tab. Click the down-arrow against the **Paper size** box to reveal the list of available paper sizes, as shown in Fig. 2.20. Change the page size to your new choice, probably A4.

Fig. 2.20 The Paper Tab Sheet of the Page Setup Box

Any changes you can make to your document from the Page Setup dialogue box can be applied to either the whole document or to the rest of the document starting from the current position of the insertion pointer. To set this, click the down-arrow button against the **Apply to** box and choose from the drop-down list. As before, click the **Set As Default** button to make your changes affect all your new documents.

The **Paper source** section of the Page Setup box lets you set where your printer takes its paper from. You might have a printer that holds paper in trays, in which case you might want to specify that the **First page** (headed paper perhaps), should be taken from one tray, while **Other pages** should be taken from a different tray.

Modifying the Page Layout

Clicking the Layout tab of the Page Setup box, displays the sheet shown in Fig. 2.21 on the next page, from which you can set options for headers and footers, section breaks, vertical alignment and whether to add line numbers or borders.

Fig. 2.21 The Layout Tab Sheet of the Page Setup Box

The default for **Section start** is 'New page' which allows the section to start at the top of the next page. Pressing the down arrow against this option, allows you to change this choice.

In the Headers and Footers section of the dialogue box, you can specify whether you want one header or footer for even-numbered pages and a different header or footer for odd-numbered pages. You can further specify if you want a different header or footer on the first page from the header or footer used for the rest of the document. Word aligns the top line with the 'Top' margin, but this can be changed with the **Vertical alignment** option.

Saving to a File

The quickest way to save a document to disc is to click the **Save** button on the Quick Access toolbar. The usual way however is from the **File** button which opens the Backstage page (see Fig. 1.8 on page 12), which gives you more control of the saving operation.

- **Save** is used when a document has previously been saved to disc in a named file; using this command saves your work under the existing filename automatically without prompting you.

- **Save As** is used when you want to save your document with a different name or file format, or in a different location.

Using the **Save As** command (or the first time you use the **Save** command when a document has no name), opens the dialogue box shown in Fig. 2.22.

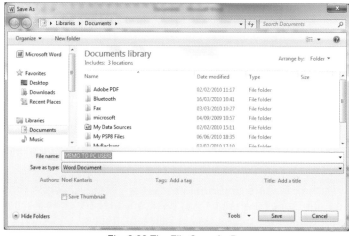

Fig. 2.22 The File Save As Box

Note that the first 255 characters of the first paragraph of a new document are placed and highlighted in the **File name** field box, with the program waiting for you to over-type a new name.

Filenames must have less than 255 characters and cannot include any of the following keyboard characters: /, \, >, <, *, ?, ", |, :, or ;. Word 2010 adds the new file extension **.docx** automatically and uses it to identify its documents.

You can select a drive other than the default C: drive, by clicking the down arrow on the left pane of the **Save As** box and navigate to an appropriate drive and folder.

We used the **New Folder** button to create a folder called **Office 2010 Docs** on our D: drive. You could create this folder in the **Libraries**, **Documents** in the C: drive, as an alternative. To save our work currently in memory, we selected this folder in the **Save in** field of the Save As dialogue box, and then moved the cursor into the **File name** box, and typed **PC User 1**. We suggest you do the same.

By clicking the **Save as type** down-arrow button at the bottom of the Save As dialogue box, you can save the Document Template, or the Text Only parts of your work, or you can save your document in a variety of formats, including Rich Text, and several Web Page options. The default is always Word Document which has the file extension **.docx**. Word 97-2003 document file type has the extension **.doc**, in case you want to send this file to a friend who does not have the latest or previous version of Word.

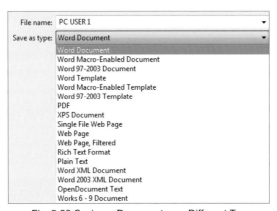

Fig. 2.23 Saving a Document as a Different Type

Selecting File Location

You can select where Word automatically looks for your document files when you first choose to open or save a document, by clicking the **File** button ![File] (to open the Backstage page), clicking the **Options** button to open the Word Options dialogue, and clicking the **Save** button on this screen to display Fig. 2.24, shown on the next page.

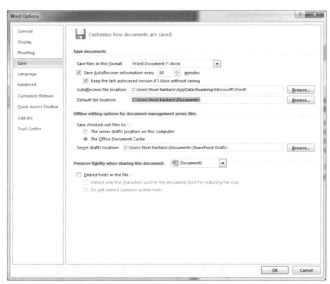

Fig. 2.24 Setting Word's File Locations

Microsoft suggests that you store documents, worksheets, presentations, and other files you are currently working on, in your personal **Documents** folder, which is easily accessed from the **Start** button. This, of course, is a matter of preference, so we leave it to you to decide. We prefer to create sub-folders within a drive partition.

Closing a Document

There are several ways to close a document in Word. Once you have saved it you can click its window close ████ button. If you only have one document open in Word this will close the program, in which case it is better to click the **File** ███ button and click the **Close** ░ Close button on the Backstage screen.

If the document (or file) has changed since the last time it was saved, you will be given the option to save it before it is removed from memory. If a document is not closed before a new document is opened, then both documents will be held in memory in their own Word windows, but only one will be the current document.

Opening a Document

To open a file in Word, either use the **Ctrl+O** keyboard shortcut or click the **File** button, and then click the **Open** button on the Backstage screen shown in Fig. 2.25. Either of these opens the screen shown in Fig. 2.26 below.

Fig. 2.25 The Open Button on the Backstage screen

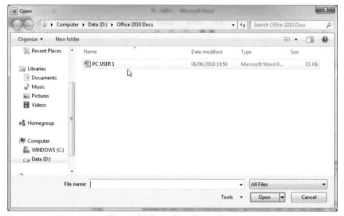

Fig. 2.26 The File Open Box

New Documents

To open a new document into Word 2010 when an existing document is already opened, click the **File** button, and then click the **Open** button on the Backstage screen. This allows you to open files that might be located at a different place from that of your default path, as shown in Fig. 2.27 on the next page.

Alternatively, click the **File** button, and then click the **New** button which displays various templates, as shown in Fig. 2.28 on the next page. From here you can select a 'Blank Document', or one of the displayed templates. On the right of the screen there is a preview panel so can see what you'll get when choosing a particular template.

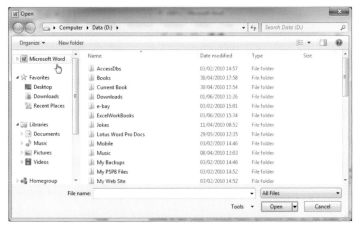

Fig. 2.27 The Microsoft Word Link

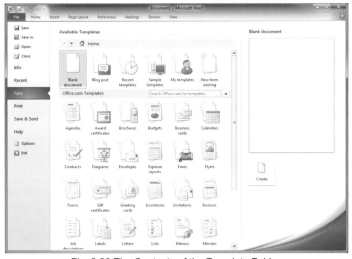

Fig. 2.28 The Contents of the Template Folder

* * *

In the next Chapter we explore how to change documents by using editing and formatting techniques which can help to enhance their content.

3

Changing Word Documents

Microsoft have built some very clever editing and formatting facilities into Word 2010. When you enter text you will notice that some basic errors are automatically corrected and that misspelled words are unobtrusively underlined in a red wavy line and ungrammatical phrases are similarly underlined in green.

AutoCorrect

To demonstrate these, start Word and in the displayed new document page, type the words '**teh compter is brukn**', exactly as misspelled here.

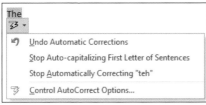

Fig. 3.1 The AutoCorrect Options Button

As soon as you press the space bar after entering the first 'word', it will be changed to 'The', as shown in Fig. 3.1. This is the **AutoCorrect** feature at work, which will automatically detect and correct many typing errors, misspelled words and incorrect capitalisation. If you agree with the change made, just carry on. If not, you can move the pointer over the corrected word until a blue box is shown below it. This changes to the **AutoCorrect Options** button when you point to it, and clicking it opens the above menu.

Selecting the first menu option **Undo Automatic Corrections** will cancel the correction for you. The other options give you control over how the feature works in the future. It is worth experimenting a bit here to find out more.

If an error cannot be corrected automatically, it will be underlined in a red wavy line. Right-clicking the misspelled word displays a list of choices from which you can select the correct word by left-clicking on it. You even have a choice of **Language** to use.

Editing Text

Other editing could include deleting unwanted words or adding extra text in the document. For small deletions, such as letters or words, use the **Del** or **BkSp** keys.

With the **Del** key, position the cursor on the left of the first letter you want to delete and press **Del**. With the **BkSp** key, position the cursor immediately to the right of the character to be deleted and press **BkSp**. In both cases the rest of the line moves to the left to take up the space created by the deleting process.

Word processing is usually carried out in the insert mode. Any characters typed will be inserted at the cursor location (insertion point) and the following text will be pushed to the right, and down, to make room. To insert blank lines in your text, place the cursor at the beginning of the line where the blank line is needed and press **Enter**. To remove the blank line, position the cursor on it and press **Del**.

When larger scale editing is needed you have several alternatives, but we only discuss here the simplest method.

 First 'select' the text to be altered (see below), then use the **Cut** ✄, **Copy** 📋 and **Paste** 📋 Ribbon controls in the Clipboard group of the Home tab, as shown here.

Selecting Text

The procedure in Word, as with most Windows based applications, is first to select the text to be altered before any operation, such as editing or formatting, can be carried out on it (use the **PC User 1** file to experiment). Selected text is highlighted on the screen. This can be carried out as follows:

- To select a block of text with keyboard – Position the cursor on the first character to be selected and hold down the **Shift** key while using the arrow keys to highlight the required text, then release the **Shift** key.

- To select the whole document – Use the **Ctrl+A** shortcut keystroke.

- To select non-contiguous text and graphics (ones that aren't next to each other), you must select the first item you want, such as a word, sentence or paragraph, hold down the **Ctrl** key and select any other items from anywhere in the document. You can only select text, or graphics in this way, not both at the same time.

Copying Blocks of Text

Once text has been selected it can be copied to another location in your present document, to another Word document, or to another Windows application, via the system Clipboard. As with most of the editing and formatting operations there are several alternative ways of doing this, as follows:

- With the mouse, use the **Copy** 📋 Ribbon control button in the Clipboard group of the Home tab, move the cursor to the start of where you want the copied text to be placed, and click the **Paste** 📋 command.

- With the keyboard, use the quick key combinations, **Ctrl+C** to copy and **Ctrl+V** to paste.

To copy the same text again to another location, or to any open document window or application, move the cursor to the new location and paste it there with either of these methods.

The above operations use the system Clipboard which in both Office 2007 and Office 2010 can store 24 cut or copied items until they are needed. Each item is displayed as an entry on the **Clipboard** Task Pane as shown in Fig. 3.2 on the next page. The previous version of Office could only hold one cut or copied item at a time.

Fig. 3.2 Pasting from the Clipboard Task Pane

The Clipboard Task Pane

To illustrate how the Clipboard contents can be used, open the **PC User 1** file (if not already opened) in Word and select the first word of each Heading line of the memo (in this case "Data", "Structure" and "Finding") and delete it using either the **Cut** control button in the Clipboard group of the Home tab, or the **Ctrl+X** key combination. Now open the **Clipboard** Task Pane by clicking the **Clipboard** button pointed to above. The **Clipboard** Task Pane in Fig. 3.2, shows three text items. Clicking an item on the Clipboard, pastes that item at the cursor position within the memo.

By default a **Smart Tag** is placed under newly pasted text in Word. Pressing the **Ctrl** key or clicking the down-arrow, displays several Paste Options. These let you control the style and formatting of the pasted text (place the mouse pointer over each to find out their function). If you don't want to make any formatting changes, just carry on and the Smart Tag will 'go away'.

Moving Blocks of Text

Selected text can be moved to any location in the same document using either of the following methods:

- Clicking the **Cut** ✂ control button.

- Using the **Ctrl+X** keyboard shortcut.

Next, move the cursor to the required new location and as described previously paste the text where you want it.

The moved text will be placed at the cursor location and will force any existing text to make room for it. This operation can be cancelled by simply pressing **Esc**. Once moved, multiple copies of the same text can be produced by other **Paste** actions.

Deleting Blocks of Text

When text is 'cut' by clicking the **Cut** ✂ Ribbon control button, it is removed from the document, but placed on the clipboard. When the **Del** or **BkSp** keys are used, however, the text is deleted but not put on the clipboard.

The Undo Command

If you make a mistake when using the delete command, all is not lost as long as you act straight away. The **Undo** keyboard shortcut, **Ctrl+Z,** reverses your most recent editing or formatting commands.

Fig. 3.3 The Undo Button

To make deeper changes you can use the **Undo** button on the Quick Action toolbar, shown here, to undo one of several editing or formatting actions (pressing the down arrow to the right of the button shows a list of your most recent changes).

Undo does not reverse any action once editing changes have been saved to file. Only editing done since the last save can be reversed.

Finding and Changing Text

Word allows you to search for specifically selected text, or character combinations with the **Find** and **Replace** options in the **Editing** group on the Home tab of the Ribbon.

Using the **Find** option (**Ctrl+F**), will highlight each occurrence of the text typed in the **Search** box of the **Navigation** pane in turn so that you can carry out some action on it, such as change its font or appearance. Using the **Replace** option (**Ctrl+H**), allows you to specify what replacement is to be automatically carried out. For example, in a long article you may decide to replace the word 'computers' with the word 'PCs'.

To illustrate the procedure, click the **Replace** button shown above, (or use the **Ctrl+H** quick key combination). This opens the Find and Replace dialogue box shown below in Fig. 3.4 with the **More** button clicked.

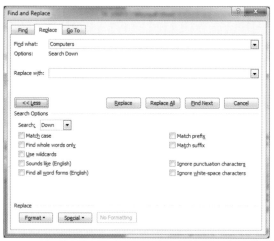

Fig. 3.4 The Find and Replace Dialogue Box

Towards the bottom of the dialogue box, there are five check boxes; the first two can be used to match the case of letters in the search string, or a whole word, while the last three are used for wildcard, 'sounds like' or 'word forms' matching.

The two buttons, **Format** and **Special**, situated at the bottom of the dialogue box, let you control how the search is carried out. Have a look at the list of available options, when either of these buttons is pressed. You can force both the search and the replace operations to work with exact text attributes. For example, selecting:

- The **Font** option from the list under **Format**, displays a dialogue box in which you select a font (such as Arial, Times New Roman, etc.); a font-style (such as regular, bold, italic, etc.); an underline option (such as single, double, etc.); and special effects (such as strike-through, superscript, subscript, etc.).

- The **Paragraph** option, lets you control indentation, spacing (before and after), and alignment.

- The **Style** option, allows you to search for, or replace, different paragraph styles. This can be useful if you develop a new style and want to change all the text of another style in a document to use your preferred style.

Using the **Special** button, you can search for, and replace, various specified document marks, tabs, hard returns, etc., or a combination of both these and text, as shown in Fig. 3.4.

Below we list only two of the many key combinations of special characters that could be typed into the **Find what** and **Replace with** boxes when the **Use wildcards** box is checked.

Type	*To find or replace*
?	Any single character within a pattern. For example, searching for nec?, will find <u>neck</u>, con<u>nect</u>, etc.
*	Any string of characters. For example, searching for c*r, will find such words as <u>cellar</u>, <u>chillier</u>, etc., also parts of words such as <u>charac</u>ter, and combinations of words such as <u>connect, cellar</u>.

The Research Task Pane

Clicking the **Research** button in the **Proofing** group of the **Review** tab, shown here, opens the **Research** Task Pane (Fig. 3.5). This facility is available with all the Office 2010 applications and allows you to reference multiple sources of information, on your computer or the Internet, without leaving an Office program.

For example, you could look up words or phrases in the Live Search UK, or any of the other available sites, which can give you definitions, word histories, pronunciation, and word usage notes. Fig. 3.6 below shows the books and research sites that were available to us.

Fig. 3.6 Research
Reference Sources

Fig. 3.5 The Research
Task Pane

Another source of information is the Thesaurus where you could look up synonyms and insert them into your document directly from the Research Task Pane.

In the list of results on the Research Task Pane, you can also click related links that take you to additional information on the Internet. You can also get translations using bilingual dictionaries on your computer or online, or get stock quotes and company information while you work. The choice is yours!

Page Breaks

Word automatically inserts a 'soft' page break in a document when a page of typed text is full. To force a manual, or hard page break, either use the **Ctrl+Enter** keyboard shortcut, or click the **Insert**, **Pages**, **Blank Page** command button on the Ribbon.

To delete manual page breaks place the cursor at the beginning of the second page and press the **BkSp** key. Soft page breaks which are automatically entered by the program at the end of pages, cannot be deleted.

Formatting Word Documents

Formatting involves the appearance of individual words or even characters, the line spacing and alignment of paragraphs, and the overall page layout of the entire document. These functions are carried out in Word in several different ways.

Primary page layout is included in a document's Template, text formatting in a Template's styles and Theme. Within any document, however, you can override Paragraph Style formats by applying text formatting and enhancements manually to selected text. To immediately cancel manual formatting, use the **Undo** button [icon] on the Quick Access toolbar, or use the **Ctrl+Z** key shortcut. The text reverts to its original format. You can cancel manual formatting by selecting the text and using the **Clear All** option in the Styles Task Pane. The text then reverts to the Normal style format.

Formatting Text

Fonts are automatically installed when you set up Windows. Originally, the title and headings of the **PC User 1** memo, were selected from the Style gallery as 'Title' and 'Heading1', which were in the default 26 and 12 point size Cambria, respectively, while the main text was typed in 11 point size Calibri.

To change this memo into what appears in Fig. 3.7 below, first select the title of the memo and format it to bold, italics, 20 point size Arial and centre it between the margins, then select the subtitles and format each to 16 point size bold Arial. Finally select each paragraph of the main body of the memo in turn, and format it to 12 point size Arial.

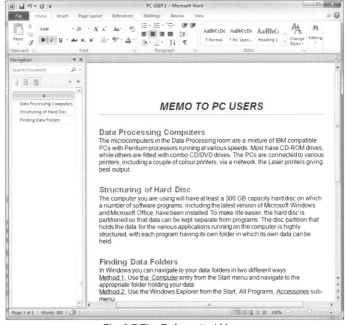

Fig. 3.7 The Reformatted Memo

All of this formatting can be achieved by using the buttons on the Ribbon or by using keyboard shortcuts, some of which are listed below:

To Format	*Type*
Bold	**Ctrl+B**
Italic	**Ctrl+I**
Underline	**Ctrl+U**
Word underline	**Ctrl+Shift+W**

There are shortcuts to do almost anything, but the ones listed here are the most useful and the easiest to remember.

Paragraph Alignment

Word defines a paragraph, as any text which is followed by a paragraph mark, which is created by pressing the Enter key. So single line titles, as well as sections of long typed text, can form paragraphs.

Word allows you to align a paragraph at the left margin (the default), at the right margin, centred between both margins, or justified between both margins.

Fig. 3.8 Paragraph Group

There are two main ways to perform alignment in Word. Using the Ribbon, **Home**, **Paragraph** command buttons, shown in Fig. 3.8, or using keyboard shortcuts.

Ribbon Buttons	*Alignment*	*Keystrokes*
≣	Left	**Ctrl+L**
≣	Centred	**Ctrl+E**
≣	Right	**Ctrl+R**
≣	Justified	**Ctrl+J**

Save the reformatted Memo to PC Users as **PC User 2**, using **Save As** command in the Backstage page.

Indenting Text

Most documents will require some form of paragraph indenting, where an indent is the space between the margin and the edge of the text in the paragraph. When an indent is set (on the left or right side of the page), any justification on that side of the page sets at the indent, not the page margin.

To illustrate indentation, open the file **PC User 2**, select the first paragraph, and use the **Decrease/Increase Indent** buttons on the Ribbon shown here.

Alternatively, open the Paragraph box by clicking the **Home**, **Paragraph** Dialogue Box Launcher. In the **Indentation** field, select 1.5 cm for both **Left** and **Right**, as shown in Fig. 3.9 below. When you click **OK**, the first selected paragraph is displayed indented on both sides, something you can not do just by using the relevant Ribbon icon which only indents the left side. Our screen dump shows the result of the indentation as well as the settings on the Paragraph dialogue box which caused it.

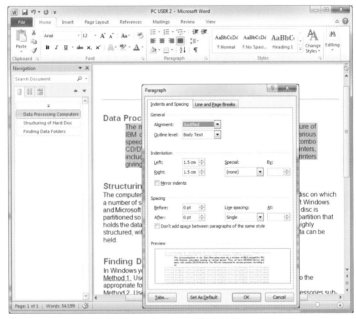

Fig. 3.9 Setting Left and Right Indentation

The **Indentation** option in the Paragraph dialogue box, can be used to create 'hanging' indents, where all the lines in a paragraph, including any text on the first line that follows a tab, are indented by a specified amount. This is often used in lists to emphasise certain points.

Next, highlight the last four lines of text in your memo, open the Paragraph dialogue box, and select 'Hanging' under **Special** and 3 cm under **By**. When you click the **OK** button, the text formats as shown in the composite screen dump of Fig. 3.10, but it is still highlighted. To remove the highlighting, click the mouse button anywhere on the page. The second and following lines of the selected paragraphs, should be indented 3 cm from the left margin.

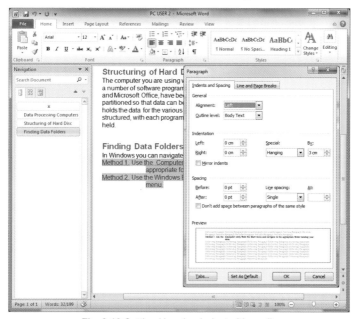

Fig. 3.10 Setting Hanging Indents Manually

This is still not very inspiring, so to complete the effect we will edit the first lines of the highlighted paragraphs as follows:

Place the cursor in front of the word 'Method 1' and press **Enter**. Then place the cursor in front of the word 'Use' and press the **Tab** key once. This places the start of the word in the same column as the indented text of the rest of that paragraph. To complete the effect, repeat the above edits on the last paragraph of the memo, as shown in Fig. 3.11 on the next page.

Fig. 3.11 Text Formatted with Hanging Indents

This may seem like a complicated rigmarole to go through each time you want the hanging indent effect, but with Word you will eventually set up all your indents, etc., as styles in templates. Then all you do is click in a paragraph to produce them. We will discuss this towards the end of this chapter, but right now save your work as **PC User 3**.

Bullets and Lists

Bullets are small characters you can insert in the text of your document to improve visual impact. In Word the main way for creating lists with bullets or numbers is from the Ribbon, **Home**, **Paragraph** group. Clicking the **Bullets** button, the **Numbering** button or the **Multilevel List** button will start the operation. You can change the bullet or list design used by clicking the down-arrow next to its button. If none of the available designs appeal to you, you can create your own by clicking **Define New Bullet** at the bottom of the box, as shown in Fig. 3.12 below.

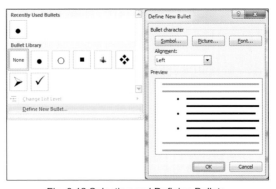

Fig. 3.12 Selecting and Defining Bullets

There are two types of bullet you can define. Clicking the **Symbol** button above lets you use a character from a font, whereas **Picture** bullets are just small graphic images. With the latter option you can select from an enormous number of bullet pictures. Very comprehensive indeed!

If you select the **Numbering** button or the **Multilevel List** button similar options are displayed, giving you a choice of several numbering or outline (multilevel) systems.

Once inserted, you can copy, move or cut a bulleted paragraph in the same way as any other text. However, you can not delete a bullet with the **BkSp** or **Del** keys. To do this, you need to place the insertion point in the line and click the **Bullets** button, shown here. Once you have set up a customised bullet, clicking this button in a paragraph will use it.

If you only want a simple list you can create it without using the Ribbon buttons. For a bulleted list, just type an asterisk '*' followed by a <u>space</u>. The asterisk turns into a bullet and your list is started. When you've finished typing the first item in your list, press the **Enter** key and a new bullet will appear on the next line.

To automatically create numbered lists in a similar way, type the number one and a full stop '**1.**', followed by a <u>space</u>.

When you have finished entering your list pressing the **Enter** key twice will close it. Every time you press the **Enter** key at the end of the list you get a new bullet or number, but if you press it again, the last bullet or number disappears.

Inserting Date and Time

You can insert today's date, the date the current document was created or was last revised, or a date or time that reflects the current system date and time into a document. Therefore, the date can be a date that changes, or a date that always stays the same. In either case, the date is inserted in a date field.

To insert a date field in your document, place the cursor where you want to insert the date, click the **Insert**, **Text**, **Date & Time** command button and choose one of the displayed date formats from the dialogue box shown in Fig. 3.13 below. This is a composite of the operation required and the result of that operation.

Fig. 3.13 Inserting Dates and Times in a Document

If you save a document with a date field in it and you open it a few days later, the date shown on it will be the original date the document was created. Most of the time this will probably be what you want, but should you want the displayed date to always update to the current date whenever the document is opened, check the **Update automatically** box in the Date and Time dialogue box, and then click the **OK** button.

Comments and Tracked Changes

Another of Word's powerful features is the facility to add comments and to track changes made to a document. These actions are all carried out from the **Review** tab.

Comments are notes, or annotations, that an author or reviewer adds to a document and in Word 2010 they are displayed in balloons in the margin of the document or in the Reviewing Pane. A tracked change is a mark that shows where a deletion, insertion or other editing change has been made in a document.

Fig. 3.14 A Comment in a Document

To quickly display or hide tracked changes or comments (known as markup) click the **Review**, **Tracking**, **Show Markup** command button, and select what you want to display on the screen. To add a comment, place the pointer in the correct location, click the **New Comment** button, and type the comment into the 'balloon' that opens in the margin. You can view a document's markup by clicking the **Reviewing Pane** command button. You can print a document with mark-ups to keep a record of any changes made.

Formatting with Page Tabs

You can format text in columns by using tab stops placed on the Ruler, opened by clicking the **View Ruler** button ☑. Although they are not shown on the Ruler, but as small marks below it, Word has default left tab stops at 1.27 cm intervals. The symbol for a left tab ⬚ appears in the tab type button at the left edge of the ruler pointed to in Fig 3.15 below.

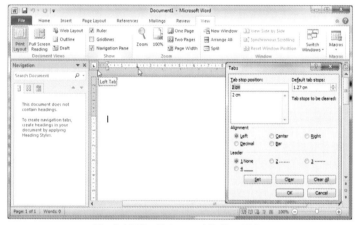

Fig. 3.15 The Rulers and Setting Tabs

To set tabs, click on the tab type button (which cycles through the available types) until the type you want is showing and then click on the ruler. To remove a tab, just drag it off the ruler.

To place tabs exactly, first set one on the Ruler (we have used a Left tab and placed it on the 2 cm mark) and then double-click it to open the Tabs dialogue box shown above.

Type the distance from the left margin for your tab in the **Tab stop position** text box and click the **Set** button. To clear the ruler of tabs press the **Clear All** button. To remove one tab, select it in the list and click the **Clear** button. Tab stops apply either to the paragraph containing the cursor, or to any selected paragraphs.

The tab stop types available have the following functions:

Button	*Name*	*Effect*
L	**Left**	Left aligns text after the tab stop.
⊥	**Centre**	Centres text on tab stop.
⅃	**Right**	Right aligns text at the tab stop.
⊥	**Decimal**	Aligns decimal point with tab stop.
I	**Bar**	Inserts a vertical line at the tab stop.

The tab type button actually cycles through two more types, first line indent 🔽 and hanging indent 🔲. These give you a quick way of adding these indents to the ruler.

If you want tabular text to be separated by characters instead of by spaces, select one of the four available characters from the **Leader** box in the Tabs dialogue box. The options are none (the default), dotted, dashed and underline. The Contents pages of this book are set with right tabs and dotted leader characters.

When you are finished click the **OK** button to make your changes active. Now using the Tab key displays the selected leader characters. If you don't like what you see, press the **Clear All** button in the Tabs dialogue box. This will take you back to the default Tab settings.

Note: As all paragraph formatting, such as tab stops, is placed at the end of a paragraph, if you want to carry the formatting of the current paragraph to the next, press **Enter**. If you don't want formatting to carry on, press the down arrow key instead.

Formatting with Styles

We saw earlier on page 27, how you can format your work using Styles, but we confined ourselves to using the default styles only. In this section we will give an overview of how to create, modify, use, and manage styles. Word's Style controls, shown in Fig. 3.16, are in the **Home**, **Styles** group.

Fig. 3.16 The Home Styles Group

A Style is a set of formatting instructions which you save so that you can use it repeatedly within a document or in different documents. A collection of Styles can be placed in a Template which could be appropriate for, say all your memos, so it can be used to preserve uniformity and save time by not having to format each paragraph individually.

Further, should you decide to change a style, all the paragraphs associated with that style can reformat automatically. To provide a pattern for shaping a final document, use a Template. By default all documents which have not been assigned a template, use the **Normal.dotm** global template.

Paragraph Styles

Styles contain paragraph and character formats and a name can be attached to these formatting instructions. From then on, applying the style name is the same as formatting that paragraph with the same instructions. With Word you can create your styles by example from the **Styles** Task Pane, which is opened

Creating a New Paragraph Style

Previously, we spent some time manually creating some hanging indents in the last few paragraphs of the **PC User 3** document. Open that document and display the **Styles** Task Pane by clicking the Dialogue Box Launcher ▣ on the **Home**, **Styles** group.

Next, place the insertion pointer in one of the previously created hanging indent paragraphs, situated at the bottom of the document and click the **New Style** button 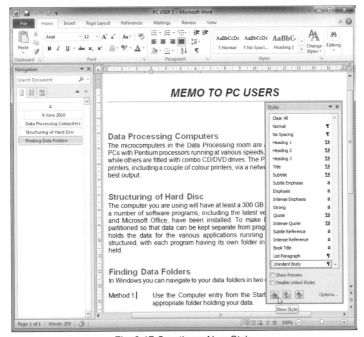 pointed to in Fig. 3.17 below.

Fig. 3.17 Creating a New Style

This opens the dialogue box shown in Fig. 3.19 on the next page. Now type the new style name you want to create in the **Name** text box, say, 'Hanging Indent', and click **OK** to accept your changes.

Finally, change the style of the other paragraphs to the new 'Hanging Indent', by selecting the new style either from the list in the **Styles** Task

Fig. 3.18 New Quick Style

Pane, or more easily, from the **Styles** gallery as shown in Fig. 3.18 above.

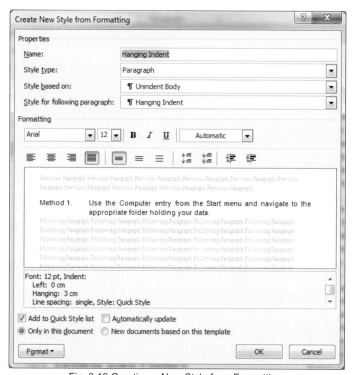

Fig. 3.19 Creating a New Style from Formatting

Save the result as **PC User 4**, but before leaving this section, have a look at some more of Word's built-in styles by clicking the **Home**, **Styles**, **Change Styles** command button, shown in Fig. 3.18 and select the **Style Set** entry from the displayed list. There are lots of available styles, one of which might suit you. As you point to each style on the list with the mouse, your document changes to give you a preview of the particular style. We leave it to you to try.

If you want some help on **Styles**, try searching for an excellent video on the subject using the Word Help system. To find it, we searched for 'Styles', then selected the 'Apply Styles in Word 2010' entry from the displayed list of topics.

You will need to be online though, as it is part of Office Online.

Document Templates

A document template provides the overall pattern of your final document. It can contain:

- Styles to control your paragraph and formats.

- A Theme to control document colours and fonts.

- Page set-up options.

- Boilerplate text, which is text that remains the same in every document.

- AutoText, which is standard text and graphics that you could insert in a document by typing the name of the AutoText entry.

- Macros, which are programs that can change the menus and key assignments to comply with the type of document you are creating.

- Customised shortcuts, toolbars and menus.

If you don't assign a template to a document, then the default **Normal.dotm** template is used by Word. To create a new document template, you either modify an existing one, create one from scratch, or create one based on the formatting of an existing document.

Creating a Document Template

To illustrate the last point above, we will create a simple document template, which we will call **PC User Memo**, based on the formatting of the **PC User 4** document. But first, make sure you have defined the 'Hanging Indent' style as explained earlier.

To create a template based on an existing document do the following:

- Open the existing document.

- Click the **File** button, and select the **Save As** command which displays the Save As dialogue box, shown in Fig. 3.20 on the next page.

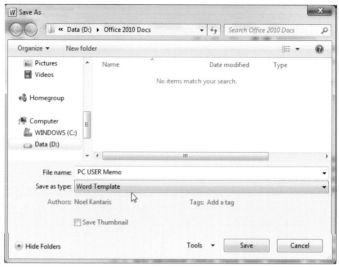

Fig. 3.20 Saving a Document as a Template

- In the **File name** box, type the name of the new template (PC USER Memo in our example). In the **Save as type** box, select **Word Template** and press the **Save** button.

- To edit your template, click the **File** button and select the **Open** command.

Fig. 3.21 Opening a Template

- Add the text and graphics you want to appear in all new documents that you base on this template, and *delete* any items (including text) you do not want.

- In our example, we deleted everything in the document, then pressed the **Enter** key several times to make room for the inserted picture and text using **Insert**, **Picture**, and **Insert**, **WordArt**, to create the screen below.

Fig. 3.22 Artwork and Text in the New Template

Note that when a picture is inserted in Word, a new tab appears on the Ribbon, which allows you to manipulate the picture without the need for any additional programs. It is worth spending sometime here to examine these additional tools which are new to this version of Word. Finally,

- Click the **File**, **Save As** command and save your creation as a 'Word Template', giving it the name 'PC User Group'.

To use the new template, do the following:

- Use the **File**, **Open** command and select 'Word Templates' as the file type you want to display, then select the required template from the list (in our case **PC User Group**).

- Type the rest of your memo, then use the **File**, **Save As** command, but this time make sure you choose 'Word Document' as the **Save as type**

Fig. 3.23 Using the New Template then Saving As a Word Document

Templates can also contain Macros as well as AutoText; macros allow you to automate Word keystroke actions only, while AutoText speeds up the addition of building blocks of text and graphics into your document. However, the design of these features is beyond the scope of this book.

Don't forget that Word has a series of built-in templates to suit 'every occasion' as we touched on in page 37. To see these, click the **File**, **New** command buttons which displays all the available Word templates with a preview of what they will look like when selected. Again, it is worth spending some time examining what is available to you.

Symbols and Special Characters

Word 2010 lets you easily add symbols to your documents. Clicking the **Symbol** command button shown below, opens a small gallery of common and recently used symbols for you to choose from. Clicking the **More Symbols** option opens the Symbol dialogue box shown in Fig. 3.24 below. From this you can select characters and symbols and insert them into your document.

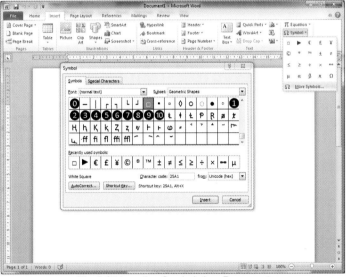

Fig. 3.24 Inserting Symbols in a Document

You should be able to find just about any symbol you require in the Symbol font box shown above. But if not, pressing the down-arrow button next to the **Font** box, will reveal the other available character sets.

If you double-click the left mouse button on a character, it transfers it to your document at the insertion point, making it extremely easy to use.

Inserting Other Special Characters

You can include other special characters in a document, such as optional hyphens, which remain invisible until they are needed to hyphenate a word at the end of a line; non-breaking hyphens, which prevent unwanted hyphenation; non-breaking spaces, which prevent two words from splitting at the end of a line; or opening and closing single quotes.

There are two ways to insert these special characters in your document. One is to click the **Special Characters** tab of the Symbol dialogue box which reveals a long list of these special characters, as shown in Fig. 3.25 below. You then select one of them and click the **Insert** button.

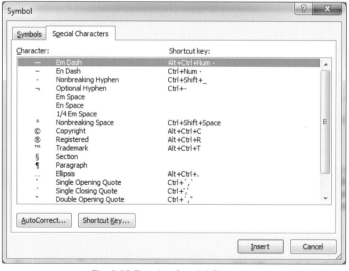

Fig. 3.25 Entering Special Characters

The other way is to use the keyboard shortcut key combinations listed above, which does not require you to open the dialogue box, but requires you to have a very good memory!

Word Web App

Microsoft Word Web App is part of Microsoft Web Apps which allows you to create Word, Excel, PowerPoint, and OneNote documents on Windows Live. This allows you to work with documents directly on the Web site where they are stored. In Microsoft Word 2010 you can start using Word Web App by saving your document to Windows Live SkyDrive. On the File Backstage page, click **Save & Send**, and then click **Save to Web**.

However, before you can use this facility, you must set up a Windows Live ID, which is very easy to do and is free! If you already use Hotmail, Messenger or Xbox Live, then you already have a Windows Live ID. If not, use your Internet Explorer and go to the www.live.com Web site. In the displayed screen, click the **Sign up** link and fill in the required information, then click the **I accept** button. It is as easy as that!

In Fig. 3.26, we show the screen prior to saving our **PC User Memo** to the Windows SkyDrive. You can even create a new folder within **My Documents** folder to keep different document types in appropriate folders. You can also use the **Save As** option to save your document by a different name.

Fig. 3.26 Saving a Document to Windows Live SkyDrive

At present the size of your SkyDrive is 25GB, so you can save quite a lot of documents. You can also allow your friends to see your documents and comment on them.

Finally, you can use the **File**, **Save & Send** command to publish a Word document to a Blog site, send it as an attachment to an e-mail (more about this later), or create a PDF (Portable Document Format) and send it to someone.

To retrieve a document from SkyDrive (from anywhere in the World), use your Internet Explorer and go to www.live.com, sign in with your Live ID and Password, click on **Office** and select **Your Documents**, **My Documents**.

Now, by clicking the required document on SkyDrive, it is loaded into Word Web App, as shown in Fig. 3.27, and then you can use the **File** command button to display a menu of options, such as Open in Word, Print, Share, etc.

Fig. 3.27 Loading a Document into Word Web App for Viewing or Printing

Clicking the **Edit in Browser** button in Fig. 3.27, opens the Word Web App and loads your document as shown in Fig. 3.28. As you can see, although the options available on the Ribbon are a limited version to those in Word, they are quite adequate. We leave it to you to explore.

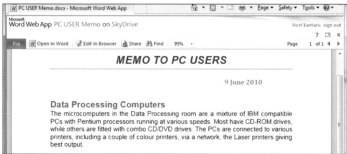

Fig. 3.28 Loading a Document into Word Web App for Editing

Printing Documents

To print a document, open it in Word, then use the **File**, **Print** command which displays the screen below.

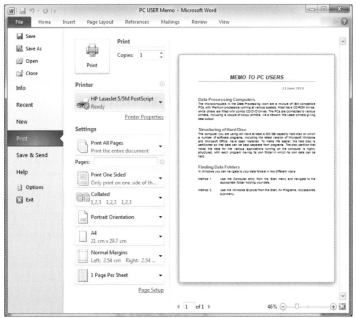

Fig. 3.29 The Print Screen

You can print a document in various ways, as follows:

- Click the **Print** button to print the document using the default printer and current settings. You can also specify the number of copies to be printed in the **Print**, **Copies** box.

- The **Settings** in the Print screen of Fig. 3.29, allow you to select which pages to print, whether one sided or not, collated or not, in Portrait or Landscape, etc. You can also click the **Page Setup** button to display the Page Setup dialogue box in which you can change Margins, Paper Size, and Print Orientation.

- In the **Printer** box you can select which printer to use, as shown for one of our computers in Fig. 3.30.

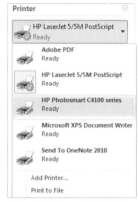

One thing to remember is that, whenever you change printers, the appearance of your document may change, as Word uses the fonts available with the newly selected printer. This can affect the line lengths, which in turn will affect both the tabulation and pagination of your document.

Fig. 3.30 New Quick Style

Throughout the process of selecting printers, etc., your document is displayed in the Preview pane to the right of the Print screen, so you can see what you'll get before committing to paper.

* * *

Word has many more features, far too numerous to mention in the space allocated to this book, although we will be discussing later how you can use Word to share information with other Microsoft applications and how to use it to add an attachment to an e-mail.

What we have tried to do so far, is give you enough basic information so that you can have the confidence to forge ahead and explore the rest of Word's capabilities by yourself.

Perhaps, you might consider exploring page numbering, headers and footers, tables, frames and drawing amongst other things. We leave it to you.

* * *

4

The Excel 2010 Spreadsheet

Excel 2010

Microsoft Excel 2010 is part of the Office 2010 suite and is fully integrated with all the other Office applications. Excel is a powerful and versatile program which has proved its usefulness over the years, not only in the business world, but with scientific and engineering users as well.

The program can emulate everything that can be done with a pencil, paper and a calculator. Thus, it is an 'electronic spreadsheet' or simply a 'spreadsheet', a name which is also used to describe it and other similar products. Excel is extremely flexible and can deal with the solution of complex problems which it can manage extremely fast. These can vary from budgeting and forecasting to the solution of complicated scientific and engineering problems.

The Ribbon, first introduced in Excel 2007, which groups tools by task and commands you most frequently use, has been updated and improved. As with all the other Office 2010 applications the new **File** button opens the Backstage full-screen interface for accessing all of the options relating to the application and the current Workbook document.

Excel 2010, just as its previous version, suports worksheets with 1,048,576 rows by 16,384 columns and an unlimited number of types of formatting in the same workbook. It also provides a Page Layout View that lets you check how your sheet will look in printed format, a formula bar which automatically re-sizes to accommodate long, complex formulae and a powerful charting engine.

Also new to Excel 2010 are the tiny charts that fit in a cell (sparklines) which help to visually trends alongside data.

Starting the Excel Program

To start Excel 2010, use the **Start**, **All Programs** command, select the **Microsoft Office** entry from the displayed menu, and click **Microsoft Excel 2010**, as shown in Fig. 4.1.

Fig. 4.1 Using the Start Menu

You can also double-click on an Excel worksheet file in a Windows folder, in which case the worksheet will be loaded into Excel at the same time.

The Excel Screen

When Excel is loaded, a 'blank' spreadsheet screen displays with a similar Title bar and Ribbon to those of Word, but with some differences, as shown below.

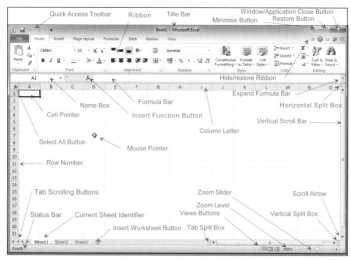

Fig. 4.2 The Excel Screen

The layout, as shown in Fig. 4.2, is in a window, but if you click on the application Restore button, you can make Excel take up the full screen area available. Working in a smaller window can be useful when you are running several applications at the same time.

The Excel window, which in this case displays an empty and untitled book (Book1), has some areas which have identical functions to those of Word (see page 18), and other areas which have different functions. Below, we describe only the areas that are exclusive to Excel.

Area	*Function*
Name box	Identifies the selected cell (by name or by cell co-ordinates), chart item, or drawing object.
Formula Bar	Can display a number, a label, or the formula behind a result.
Expand Formula Bar	Click to expand the Formula Bar.
Insert Function	Click to open the Insert Function dialogue box.
Select All Button	Click to select the whole worksheet.
Cell pointer	Marks the current cell.
Column letter	The letter that identifies each column.
Row number	The number that identifies each row.
Tab Scrolling Buttons	Clicking on these buttons, scrolls sheet tabs right or left, when there are more tabs than can be displayed at once.
Insert Worksheet	Click to insert another worksheet.
Tab split box	The split box which you drag left to see more of the scroll bar, or right to see more tabs.

Current sheet   Shows the current sheet amongst a number of sheets in a file. These are named Sheet1, Sheet2, Sheet3, and so on, by default, but can be changed to, say, North, South, East, and West. To move to a particular sheet, click its tab.

Finally, note the location of the horizontal and vertical split boxes. The first is located at the extreme right of the screen above the 'top vertical scroll arrow' button. The second is located at the extreme bottom-right corner of the screen, to the left of the 'right horizontal scroll arrow' button.

The Ribbon

The Excel Ribbon has seven tabs, each one with the most used controls grouped on it for the main program actions. For a general description of the Ribbon, see page 5.

Fig. 4.3 The Home Tab of the Excel 2010 Ribbon

A quick look at the Home tab, shows that it contains groups for the more common worksheet activities. The Clipboard cut and paste commands, Font, Alignment, Number Styles and Cells groups for manipulating cells and their contents, and Editing for other worksheet tasks.

Clicking a new tab opens a new series of groups, each with its relevant command buttons. The content of the other tabs allow you to do the following:

•   The Insert tab, enables you to immediately insert Tables, Illustrations, Charts, Links, and Text based features.

•   The Page Layout tab allows you to set your Themes, Page Setup, Scale to Fit, Sheet Options and to Arrange and group sheets.

- The Formula tab allows you to add and control formulas, consisting of a Function Library, Defined Names, Formula Auditing and sheet Calculation options.

- The Data tab groups the actions used for handling and analysing your data. These include Get External Data from various sources, Connections for handling external links, Sort & Filter selected data, Data Tools and working with an Outline so that joined cells can be collapsed and expanded.

- The Review tab groups controls for Proofing your worksheets and to initiate and track document review and approval processes. It lets you deal with Comments, and control how Changes made to a worksheet will be handled.

- The View tab allows you to set what you see on the screen. You can choose between Worksheet Views, Show or Hide screen features, Zoom to different magnifications, control Windows and run and record Macros.

Workbook Navigation

When you first enter Excel, it sets up a series of worksheets, in your computer's memory, many times larger than the small part shown on the screen. Individual cells are identified by column and row location (in that order), with present size extending to 16,384 columns and 1,048,576 rows. The columns are labelled from A to Z, followed by AA to AZ, BA to BZ, and so on, to XFD, while the rows are numbered from 1 to 1048576.

The point where a row and column intersect is called a cell, and the reference points of a cell are known as the cell address. The active cell (A1 at first) is boxed.

With the large increase in the possible size of Excel 2010's worksheets, finding your way around them is even more important than it used to be.

There are four main ways of moving around a worksheet: The **Go To** box, scrolling with the mouse, using the scroll bars, or using key combinations.

The Go To Box

Pressing the **F5** function key will display the **Go To** dialogue box shown in Fig. 4.4.

In the **Go to** box a list of named ranges in the active worksheet (to be discussed shortly) is displayed, or one of the last four references from which you chose the **Go To** command.

In the **Reference** text box you type the cell reference or a named range you want to move to.

Fig. 4.4 The Go To Box

Mouse Scrolling

If you have a mouse with a wheel, such as a Microsoft IntelliMouse, you will be able to move easily around Excel 2010's enormous worksheets, as follows:

* To scroll up or down: Rotate the wheel forward or back.

* To pan through a worksheet: Hold down the wheel button, and drag the pointer away from the origin mark in any direction that you want to scroll.

* To zoom in or out: Hold down **Ctrl** while you rotate the mouse wheel forward or back. The percentage of the zoomed worksheet is displayed on the status bar.

Using the Scroll Bars

* To scroll one row up or down: Click the ▲ or ▼ scroll arrows on the vertical scroll bar.

* To scroll one column left or right: Click the ◄ or ► scroll arrows on the horizontal scroll bar.

- To scroll one window up or down: Click above or below the scroll box on the vertical scroll bar.

- To scroll one window left or right: Click to the left or right of the scroll box on the horizontal scroll bar.

Key Combinations

- To scroll to the start and end of ranges: Press **Ctrl+→**, **Ctrl+←**, **Ctrl+↓** or **Ctrl+↑** to scroll to the start and end of each range in a column or row before stopping at the end of the worksheet.

- To scroll one window up or down: Press **PgUp** or **PgDn**.

- To scroll one window left or right: Press **Scroll Lock**, then **Ctrl←** or **Ctrl→**.

To use the arrow keys to move between cells, you must turn **Scroll Lock** off.

When you have finished navigating around the worksheet, press the **Ctrl+Home** key combination which will move the active cell to the A1 position (provided you have not fixed titles in any rows or columns or have no hidden rows or columns – more about these later).

The area within which you can move the active cell is referred to as the working area of the worksheet, while the letters and numbers in the border at the top and left of the working area give the 'co-ordinates' of the cells in a worksheet. The location of the active cell is constantly monitored by the 'selection indicator' in the Name Box. As the active cell is moved, this indicator displays its address, as shown in Fig. 4.5 below.

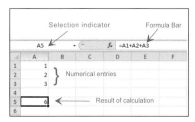

Fig. 4.5 The Selection Indicator and Formula Bar

The contents of a cell are displayed above the column letters within the 'Formula Bar'. If you type text in the active cell, it appears in both the Formula Bar and the cell itself.

Typing a formula which is preceded by the equals sign (=) to, say, add the contents of three cells, causes the actual formula to appear in the Formula Bar, while the result of the actual calculation appears in the active cell when the **Enter** key is pressed.

Moving Between Sheets

You can scroll between worksheets by clicking one of the 'Tab scrolling buttons' situated to the left of Sheet1, as shown below. The inner arrows scroll sheets one at a time in the direction of the arrow, while the outer arrows scroll to the end, or beginning, of the group of available worksheets. A worksheet is then made current by clicking its tab.

Fig. 4.6 Tab Scrolling Buttons and the Active Sheet

To display more sheet tabs at a time, drag the Tab split box to the right, or to the left to display less sheet tabs. To rename sheets, double-click on their tab, then type the new name to replace the highlighted name.

To insert a sheet, click the **Insert Worksheet** button and drag the new tab to where you want it in the stack (see the next section on the next page).

To delete a sheet, right-click on its tab and select **Delete** from the context menu shown in Fig. 4.7. As you can see, you can also **Insert**, **Rename** and **Move** or **Copy** sheets this way.

Fig. 4.7 Right-click Context Menu

Rearranging Sheet Order

To rearrange the order in which sheets are being held in a workbook, drag the particular sheet (point to it and with the left mouse button depressed move the mouse pointer) in the required direction, as shown in Fig. 4.8.

Fig. 4.8 Moving an Active Sheet

While you are dragging the tab of the sheet you want to move, the mouse pointer changes to an arrow pointing to an image of a sheet. The small solid arrowhead to the left of the mouse pointer indicates the place where the sheet you are moving will be placed.

Grouping Worksheets

You can select several sheets to group them together so that data entry, editing or formatting can be made easier and more consistent.

To select adjacent sheets, click the first sheet tab, hold down the **Shift** key and then click the last sheet tab in the group. To select non-adjacent sheets, click the first sheet tab, hold down the **Ctrl** key and then click the other sheet tabs you want to group together.

Selecting sheets in the above manner, causes the word '[Group]' to appear in the Title bar of the active window, and the tabs of the selected sheets to be shown in white. To cancel the selection, right-click a group tab and select **Ungroup Sheets**, or click the tab of any sheet which is not part of the selected group.

Selecting a Range of Cells

To select a range of cells, say, A3:C3, point to cell A3, press the left mouse button, and while holding it pressed, drag the mouse to the right.

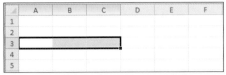

Fig. 4.9 Selecting a Range of Cells

To select a range from the keyboard, first make active the first cell in the range, then hold down the **Shift** key and use the right arrow key ($\rightarrow$) to highlight the required range.

To select a 3D range across several sheets, select the range in the first sheet, then release the mouse button, hold down the **Shift** key, and click the Tab of the last sheet in the range.

Context Menus

Excel, like all the Office 2010 programs, lets you right-click on almost anything on the screen to open a 'context' menu of actions you can take.

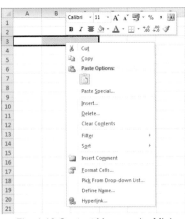

Fig. 4.10 Context Menu and a Mini Toolbar

Fig. 4.10 shows the menu options available when we right-clicked a selected range of cells. It contains the most common commands you may want to carry out. Shown above this is the Mini Toolbar, an Office feature, which contains mostly formatting controls that you can instantly carry out.

Entering Information

We will now investigate how information can be entered into a worksheet. But first, make sure you are in Sheet1, then return to the Home (A1) position, by pressing the **Ctrl+Home** key combination, then type the words:

    Project Analysis

As you type, the characters appear in both the 'Formula Bar' and the active cell. If you make a mistake, press the **BkSp** key to erase the previous letter or the **Esc** key to start again. When you have finished, press **Enter** to move to the cell below, or the **Tab** key to move to the next cell to the right.

Note that what you have just typed in has been entered in cell A1, even though the whole of the word 'Analysis' appears to be in cell B1. If you use the right arrow key to move the active cell to B1 you will see that the cell is indeed empty.

Typing any letter at the beginning of an entry into a cell results in a 'text' entry being formed automatically, otherwise known as a 'label'. If the length of the text is longer than the width of a cell, it will continue into the next cell to the right of the current active cell, provided that cell is empty, otherwise the displayed information will be truncated.

To edit information already in a cell, either

*   double-click the cell in question, or

*   make that cell the active cell and press the **F2** function key.

The cursor keys, the **Home** and **End** keys, as well as the **Ins** and **Del** keys can be used to move the cursor and/or edit information as required. You can also 'undo' the last 16 actions carried out since the program was last in the **Ready** mode, using the **Undo** button ↶▾ on the Quick Access toolbar (see page 72), or the **Ctrl+Z** keyboard shortcut.

Before you proceed, delete any information that might be in Sheet1 of your workbook by selecting it and pressing **Del**.

Next, move the active cell to B3 and type

`Jan`

Pressing the right arrow key (→) will automatically enter the typed information into the cell and also move the active cell one cell to the right, in this case to C3. Now type

`Feb`

and press **Enter**.

The looks of a worksheet can be enhanced somewhat by using different types of borders around specific cells. To do this, first select the range of cells, then click the down arrow of the **Home**, **Font**, **Borders** button which, as shown here, opens an extensive list of border types. In our example, we have selected the cell range A3:C3, then we chose the **Top and Double Bottom** Border option from the displayed table.

Fig. 4.11 The Border Button

Next, move to cell A4 and type the label **Income**, then enter the numbers **14000** and **15000** in cells B4 and C4, respectively, as shown below. Do note that by default, the labels **Jan** and **Feb** are left justified, while the numbers are right justified.

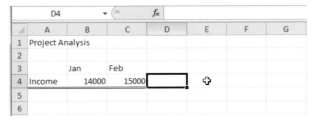

Fig. 4.12 Default Justification of Labels and Numbers

Changing Text Alignment and Fonts

Fig. 4.13 The
Alignment
Group

One way of improving the looks of this worksheet is to also right justify the text **Jan** and **Feb** within their respective cells. To do this, move the active cell to B3 and select the range B3 to C3, then click the **Home**, **Alignment**, **Align Text Right** command button, pointed to here.

For more control you can use the Format Cells dialogue box shown in Fig. 4.14 below. This is opened by clicking the **Alignment** Dialogue Box Launcher 🔲. In its Alignment tab sheet select **Right (Indent)** in the **Horizontal** drop-down list and press the **OK** button.

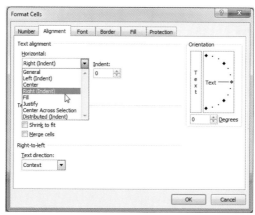

Fig. 4.14 Formatting Cells using the Alignment Tab Sheet

No matter which method you choose, the text entries should now appear right justified within their cells. The second method provides greater flexibility in displaying text, both in terms of position and orientation.

Fig. 4.15 The Font
Group

To improve the looks of our work, select cell A1, then click on the down arrow against the **Home**, **Font**, **Font Size** button on the Ribbon, and choose point size 14 from the displayed list, then click both the **Bold** and **Italic** buttons, shown in Fig. 4.15.

Fig. 4.16 Setting
Currency Format

Finally, since the numbers in cells B4 to C4 represent money, it would be better if these were prefixed with the £ sign. To do this, select the cell range B4:C4, and click the **Home**, **Number**, **Accounting Number Format** button, shown here in Fig. 4.16, and select **£ English (U.K.)**.

The numbers within the chosen range will now be displayed in currency form, and the width of the cells will automatically adjust to accommodate them, if they are too long which is the case in our example.

Fig. 4.17 Finding the Width of a Cell

To see the actual new width of, say column C, place the mouse pointer to the right of the column letter on the dividing line. When the mouse pointer changes to the shape shown here in Fig. 4.17, press the left mouse button without moving the mouse. The cell width will then display within a pop-up text box as 81 pixels, increased from the default column width of 64 pixels. To widen a column, drag the pointer to the right, until the required width is reached.

Filling in a Worksheet

We will use the few entries we have created so far (if you haven't got them, don't worry as you could just as easily start afresh, but refer to formatting made to those entries), to create the worksheet shown in Fig. 4.18 on the next page.

The lines, like the double line at the bottom of the A3 to E3 and A4 to E4 ranges were entered by first selecting each range, then right-clicking it and using the **Borders** button on the Mini Toolbar that hovers over the selection, as discussed on page 80. A super feature, this!

Alternatively, you could use the Ribbon by clicking the down-arrow of the **Home**, **Font**, **Borders** button, and selecting the appropriate border, as discussed on page 82.

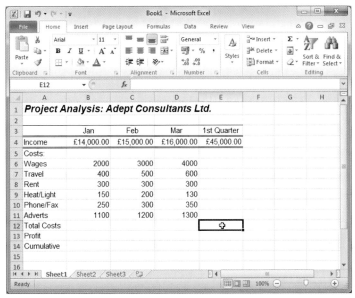

Fig. 4.18 Entering Data in a Worksheet

Formatting Entries

Fig. 4.19 Home, Font Group

The information in cell A1 (Project Analysis: Adept Consultants Ltd.) was entered left-justified and formatted from the **Home**, **Font** group by selecting Arial from the drop-down **Font** list, and 14 from the drop-down **Font Size** list, and then clicking in succession the **Bold** and **Italic** buttons, as shown above.

The text in the cell block B3:E3 was formatted by first selecting the range and then clicking the **Home**, **Alignment**, **Center** command button, shown here, to display the text in the range centre-justified.

The numbers within the cell block B4:E4 were formatted, as discussed earlier, by first selecting the range, then clicking the **Home**, **Number**, **Accounting Number Format** button, and selecting **£ English (U.K.)** from the drop-down list.

All the text appearing in column A (apart from that in cell A1) was just typed in (left justified), and formatted in Arial 11 font size. The width of all the columns A to E was adjusted to 12 characters; a quick way of doing this is to select one row of these columns, then click the **Home**, **Cells**, **Format** button, select **Column Width** from the displayed menu, type 12 in the displayed box, and click **OK**.

Filling a Range by Example

To fill a range by example, select the first cell of a range, point at the bottom right corner of the cell and when the mouse pointer changes to a small cross, as in Fig. 4.20,

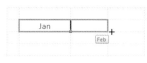

drag the mouse in the required direction to fill the range.

In the this case, we started with a cell containing the abbreviation 'Jan'. The next cell to the right will automatically fill

Fig. 4.20 Dragging a Range

with the text 'Feb' (Excel anticipates that you want to fill cells by example with the abbreviations for months, and does it for you). Not only that, but it also copies the format of the selected range forward.

The Auto Fill Smart Tag

When you release the mouse button, Excel places a Smart Tag next to the end of the filled-in range. Clicking the down-arrow of this Smart Tag displays a drop-down menu of options, as shown in Fig. 4.21.

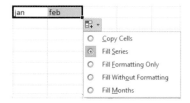

Fig. 4.21 The Auto Fill Smart Tag Options

Entering Text, Numbers and Formulas

Excel 2010 allows you to format both text (labels) and numbers in any way you choose. For example, you can have numbers centre justified in their cells.

When text, a number, a formula (see page 95), or an Excel function is entered into a cell, or reference is made to the contents of a cell by the cell address, then the content of the status bar changes from **Ready** to **Enter**. This status can be changed back to **Ready** by either completing an entry and pressing **Enter**, **Tab**, one of the arrow keys, or pressing **Esc**.

We can find the 1st quarter total income from consultancy, by activating cell E4, typing

=b4+c4+d4

and pressing **Enter**. The total first quarter income is added, using the above formula, and the result (£45,000) is placed in cell E4.

When you have entered everything in Fig. 4.18 it is time to save the work entered so far before going on any further.

Saving a Workbook

Now, let's assume we want to stop at this point, but would like to save the work entered so far before leaving the program. First, it's a good idea to return to the Home position by pressing **Ctrl+Home**. This is good practice because the position of the cell pointer at the time of saving the file is preserved.

The quickest way to save a document to disc is to click the **Save** button on the **Quick Access** toolbar. If this is the first time you use this facility, you will be asked to provide a filename and a location. The usual way, however, is to click the **File** button and select the **Save As** command from the displayed Backstage screen, which gives you more control on the saving operation, as shown in Fig. 4.22 on the next page.

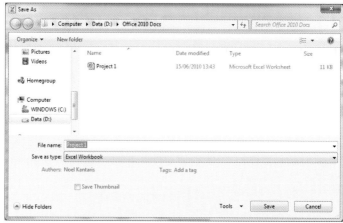

Fig. 4.22 Saving a Workbook

Above we show the action (giving our workbook the filename **Project 1**), and the result of that action. If you click the down-arrow against the **Save as type** box, you'll see the full list of available saving options, as shown in Fig. 4.23.

Fig. 4.23 Saving Options from the File Button

Using Functions

In our example, writing a formula that adds the contents of three columns is not too difficult or lengthy a task. But imagine having to add 20 columns! For this reason Excel has an inbuilt summation function which can be used to add any number of columns (or rows).

To illustrate how this and other functions can be used, activate cell E4 of **Project 1** and first, press **Del** to clear the cell of its formula, then click the **Insert Function** button in the **Function Library** group of the **Formulas** tab, shown here.

If the function you require appears on the displayed dialogue box under **Select a function**, choose it, otherwise type a brief description of what you want to do in the **Search for a function** text box and press **Go**, or select the appropriate class from the list under **Or select a category**.

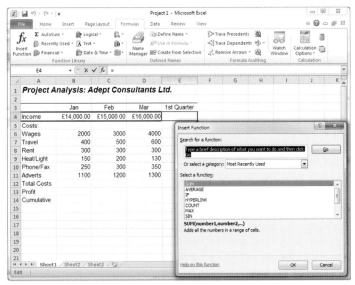

Fig. 4.24 Selecting a Function

Choosing the **SUM** function, inserts the entry SUM(B4:D4) in the Formula bar, as shown in Fig. 4.25 below. Clicking the **OK** button, places the result of the calculation of the chosen function in the selected worksheet cell. (E4 in our case).

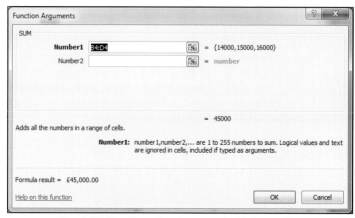

Fig. 4.25 The Function Arguments Dialogue Box

Note that the arguments in the above case are given as B4:D4 in the **Number1** box and the actual result of the calculation is displayed underneath. Pressing the **OK** button, causes the function to be pasted into cell E4, but only the formula result is displayed in the cell. If you click in the **Number2** box you can select another cell range to be summed. The overall result appears at the bottom of the box.

The AutoSum Button

With addition, there is a better and quicker way of letting Excel work out the desired result. To illustrate this, select the cell range B6:E12, which contains the 'Costs' we would like to add up. To add these in both the horizontal and vertical directions, we include in the selected range an empty column to the right of the numbers and an empty row below the numbers, as shown in Fig. 4.26 on the next page.

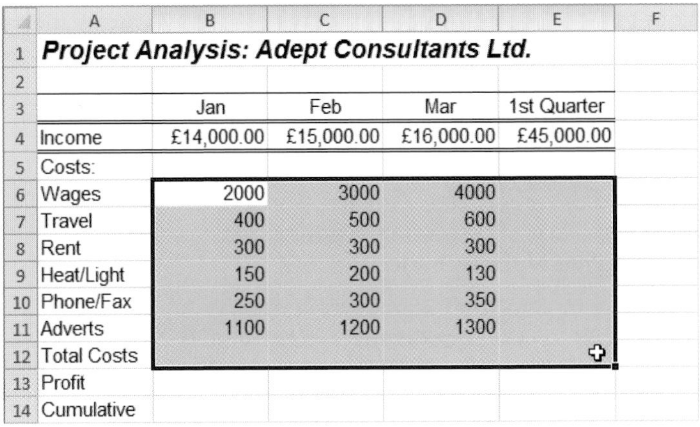

	A	B	C	D	E	F
1	**Project Analysis: Adept Consultants Ltd.**					
2						
3		Jan	Feb	Mar	1st Quarter	
4	Income	£14,000.00	£15,000.00	£16,000.00	£45,000.00	
5	Costs:					
6	Wages	2000	3000	4000		
7	Travel	400	500	600		
8	Rent	300	300	300		
9	Heat/Light	150	200	130		
10	Phone/Fax	250	300	350		
11	Adverts	1100	1200	1300		
12	Total Costs				⇩	
13	Profit					
14	Cumulative					

Fig. 4.26 Selecting the Range to be Summed

Pressing the **Formulas**, **Function Library**, **AutoSum** command button, shown on the previous page, inserts the result of the summations in the empty column and row, as shown in Fig. 4.27.

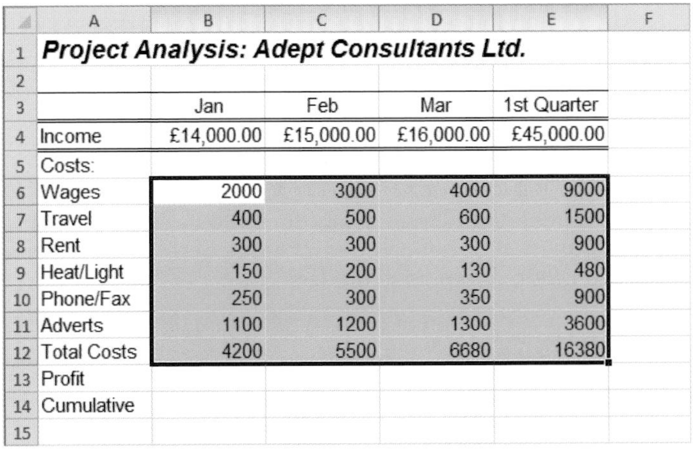

	A	B	C	D	E	F
1	**Project Analysis: Adept Consultants Ltd.**					
2						
3		Jan	Feb	Mar	1st Quarter	
4	Income	£14,000.00	£15,000.00	£16,000.00	£45,000.00	
5	Costs:					
6	Wages	2000	3000	4000	9000	
7	Travel	400	500	600	1500	
8	Rent	300	300	300	900	
9	Heat/Light	150	200	130	480	
10	Phone/Fax	250	300	350	900	
11	Adverts	1100	1200	1300	3600	
12	Total Costs	4200	5500	6680	16380	
13	Profit					
14	Cumulative					
15						

Fig. 4.27 The Result of the AutoSum Action

The selected range remains selected so that any other formatting can be applied by simply pressing the appropriate Ribbon buttons.

Note that the **AutoSum** button now has a down-arrow to the right of it. Clicking this arrow, displays a list of alternative options, as shown in Fig. 4.28. From this list you can choose to calculate the **Average**, **Count Numbers** in the entries, find the **Max** or **Min** values in a row or column, or open the Insert Function dialogue box discussed earlier by selecting the **More Functions** option.

Fig. 4.28
AutoSum Menu

Now complete the insertion of formulae in the rest of the worksheet, noting that 'Profit', in B13, is the difference between 'Income' and 'Total Cost', calculated by the formula **=b4-b12**. To complete the entry, this formula should be copied using the 'fill by example' method we discussed earlier, into the three cells to its right.

The 'Cumulative' entry in cell B14 should be a simple reference to cell B13, that is **=b13**, while in cell C14 it should be **=b14+c13**. Similarly, the latter formula is copied into cell D14 using the 'fill by example' method.

Next, format the entire range B6:E12 by selecting the range and clicking the **Home**, **Number**, **Accounting Number Format** button, shown here, and selecting **£ English (U.K.)**

If you make any mistakes and copy formats or information into cells you did not mean to, use the **Undo** button on the **Quick Access** toolbar, or the **Ctrl+Z** keyboard shortcut. To blank the contents of a range of cells, select the range, then press the **Del** key.

The data in your worksheet, up to this point, should look like that in Fig. 4.29 on the next page.

Finally, use the **Save As** button on the Backstage screen to save the resultant worksheet with the filename **Project 2**. We saved our Workbook in our **Office 2010 Docs** folder on the D: drive.

⊿	A	B	C	D	E	F
1	**Project Analysis: Adept Consultants Ltd.**					
2						
3		Jan	Feb	Mar	1st Quarter	
4	Income	£14,000.00	£15,000.00	£16,000.00	£45,000.00	
5	Costs:					
6	Wages	£ 2,000.00	£ 3,000.00	£ 4,000.00	£ 9,000.00	
7	Travel	£ 400.00	£ 500.00	£ 600.00	£ 1,500.00	
8	Rent	£ 300.00	£ 300.00	£ 300.00	£ 900.00	
9	Heat/Light	£ 150.00	£ 200.00	£ 130.00	£ 480.00	
10	Phone/Fax	£ 250.00	£ 300.00	£ 350.00	£ 900.00	
11	Adverts	£ 1,100.00	£ 1,200.00	£ 1,300.00	£ 3,600.00	
12	Total Costs	£ 4,200.00	£ 5,500.00	£ 6,680.00	£16,380.00	
13	Profit	£ 9,800.00	£ 9,500.00	£ 9,320.00	£28,620.00	
14	Cumulative	£ 9,800.00	£19,300.00	£28,620.00		
15						

Fig. 4.29 The Completed 1st Quarter Worksheet

Formulae and Functions

As we have seen, **Formulas** in Excel (or formulae to the rest of us!) are equations that perform calculations on values in your worksheet. A formula starts with an equal sign (=) and can contain any of the following:

- **Function**s – Built-in Excel formulas that take a value or values, perform an operation and return a value or values. You use functions to simplify and shorten worksheet formulas.

- **References** – Addresses of cells in the worksheet.

- **Operators** – Signs or symbols that specify the type of calculation to perform in an expression. Operators can be mathematical, comparison, logical or reference.

- **Constants** – Values that are not calculated and, therefore, do not change.

Excel Functions

Excel's functions are built-in formulas that perform specialised calculations. Their general format is:

   NAME(arg1, arg2, ...)

where **NAME** is the function name, and **arg1**, **arg2**, etc., are the arguments required for the evaluation of the function. Arguments must appear in a parenthesised list as shown above and their exact number depends on the function being used. However, some functions, such as **PI**, do not require arguments and are used without parentheses.

There are four types of arguments used with functions: numeric values, range values, string values and conditions, the type used being dependent on the type of function. Numeric value arguments can be entered either directly as numbers, as a cell address, a cell range name or as a formula. Range value arguments can be entered either as a range address or a range name, while string value arguments can be entered as an actual value (a string in double quotes), as a cell address, a cell name, or a formula. Condition arguments normally use logical operators or refer to an address containing a logic formula.

Excel has many types of functions, including, financial, logical, text, date and time, lookup and reference, mathematical and trigonometric, statistical, database, engineering and information. Each type requires its own number and type of arguments.

To find out in detail about all of Excel 2010's functions go to the **Function reference** section in Excel Help. This gives working examples of everything, but you must be online to receive them.

In Excel 2010 you can use the **Formulas** tab to place and work with formulas and functions. As shown in Fig. 4.30 on the next page, the main function types have their own Ribbon buttons (to see these as they are displayed, maximise the Excel window). Just clicking these and pointing to a function on one of their lists, gives you a good overview of what the function does and what parameters it needs.

Fig. 4.30 The Formulas, Function Library

That's enough theory, if you want to go deeper you can study the Help system.

Building a Formula

You can enter formulas straight into a selected cell, or into the Formula bar, which is now re-sizeable. In Fig. 4.31 we will step through the procedure of building a simple formula in cell D3, to average the contents of cells B2 to B4, normally refered to as the range (B2:B4).

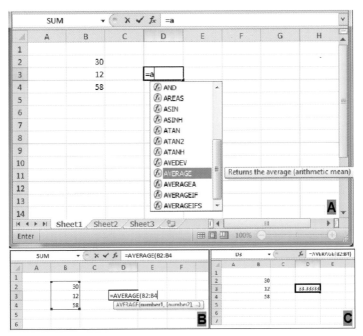

Fig. 4.31 Building a Simple Formula with a Function

In **A** (see previous page), we typed '=a' into cell D3. Excel, expecting a formula, opened the drop-down list for us to select one. This is the Formula AutoComplete feature which helps you write the proper formula syntax.

We double-clicked on **AVERAGE** and selected the range B2:B4 with the pointer, which as you can see in **B** on the previous page, entered the function and the selected range into the formula, with a syntax pop-up below to help. Pressing the **Enter** key completed the operation.

The result is shown in the cell and the completed formula in the Formula bar when the cell is selected, as shown in **C** of Fig. 4.31 on the previous page. Microsoft have made function use in Excel as intuitive as possible.

Printing a Worksheet

Before we tell you any more about worksheets, you might like to print **Project 2** to see how it looks on paper.

The quickest way of printing your work is to load the worksheet you want to print into Excel, click the **File** button, then click the **Print** button to display the screen shown in Fig. 4.32 below.

Fig. 4.32 Print Menu Options

Note the **Preview** pane on the right of the displayed screen. What you see here is dependent on the selected printer. You can also change the number of copies to be printed, the settings, the orientation and paper size.

Use the **Zoom to page** button, to be found at the bottom right corner of the Print screen, to get the best view of your work and, if you are happy with it, click the **Print** button to send your spreadsheet to the selected printer, provided your printer is connected and switched on.

The idea of the **Preview** pane is to make it easy for you to see your work on screen before committing it to paper, thus saving a few trees and a lot of ink!

Next, we discuss in much more detail how to **Print** large spreadsheets, how to use **Page Setup** to transform your printout to your liking, and how to use headers and footers.

Printing a Large Worksheet

Fig. 4.33 The Page Setup Group

Before you print from a large worksheet you should check and if necessary change the print settings. Most of the commands for this are in the **Page Layout**, **Page Setup** group shown in Fig. 4.33.

Setting a Print Area

To choose a smaller print area than the current worksheet, select the required area by highlighting the starting cell of the area and dragging the mouse to highlight the block, click the **Print Area** command button selected above, and choose the **Set Print Area** option on the drop-down menu.

As an example, open the **Project 2** file, if not already opened, and set the print range as A1:E14. Next, click the View tab and click the **Page Layout** button shown here. This opens the screen shown in Fig. 4.34 on the next page, with the View tab open.

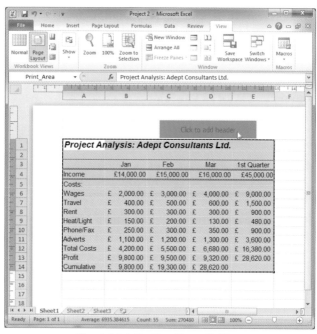

Fig. 4.34 Adjusting Page Settings

Clicking the area pointed to in Fig. 4.34, allows you to add a header. Doing so, Excel displays a contextual tab, shown in Fig. 4.35 below.

Fig. 4.35 The Contextual Header and Footer Tab

From here, you can navigate to the Header or Footer, add page numbers, current date, etc., very quickly. It is worth spending some time examining the facilities offered within this tab, but we leave it to you to explore by yourself.

Nevertheless, in the next chapter we shall be discussing an alternative method of adding Header and Footer information into a spreadsheet. As always, there is more than one way of achieving the same goal!

5

Enhancing Excel Worksheets

Opening an Excel File

To open a previously saved file in Excel, select it from the **Recent** list, or click the **File** button, then click the **Open** button on the Backstage screen, or use the **Ctrl+O** keyboard shortcut. All of these launch the Open dialogue box, shown in Fig. 5.1 below. Excel asks for a filename to open, with the default *All Excel Files* being displayed in the **Files of type** box.

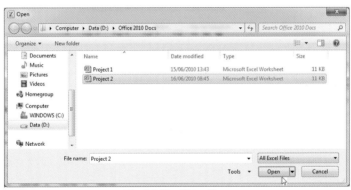

Fig. 5.1 The Open Box

To open our previously saved example, **Project 2**, navigate to where you saved it (in our example in drive D:, in the **Office 2010 Docs** folder), select it by clicking its name in the list box, then click the **Open** button.

In what follows, we will use the contents to **Project 2** to show you how to apply enhancements to it, and eventually how to create 3-D worksheets and how to create professional looking charts from your data.

Applying Enhancements to a Worksheet

You can make your work look more professional by adopting various enhancements, such as single and double line cell borders, shading certain cells and adding meaningful headers and footers.

Formatting Cells

With Excel 2010 it is easy to enhance cells by colouring them appropriately. To do this, select the range you want to format, say A5:A14, then click the **Format** button on the **Home**, **Cells** group, and select **Format Cells** from the displayed menu, as shown in Fig. 5.2.

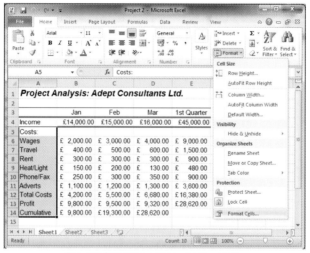

Fig. 5.2 Selecting and Formatting Cells

This opens the Format Cells dialogue box with a number of tabs which can be used to apply different types of formatting to cells. Using the Fill tab and clicking the **Fill Effects** button, opens a similarly named dialogue box in which you can select one or two colours, the shading styles and variants of your preference. We selected a pinkish colour for all the **Costs** labels (A5:A14), and repeated the process, but this time gave the **Income** labels (A3:E4) a bluish tint.

Below we show the Format Cells and Fill Effects screens in a composite display in Fig. 5.3.

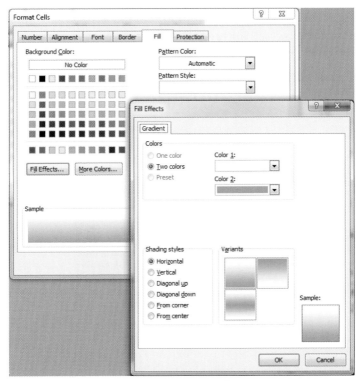

Fig. 5.3 Selecting Fill Effects

Next, reduce the title of the worksheet to 'Project Analysis', then centre it within the range A1:E1, by first selecting the range, then clicking the **Home**, **Alignment**, **Merge** button and selecting **Merge and Centre**, as shown in Fig. 5.4. This centres the title within the selected range. Finally, save the worksheet as **Project 3**, before going on.

Fig. 5.4 Selecting the Merge & Center Alignment option

Next, highlight the cell range A1:E14 and select the width as **1 page** from the **Scale to Fit** group of the **Page Layout** tab on the Ribbon. Finally, with the same cell selection, click the down-arrow against **Accounting** in the **Home**, **Number** group and select **Currency** from the drop-down menu, as shown in Fig. 5.5 below.

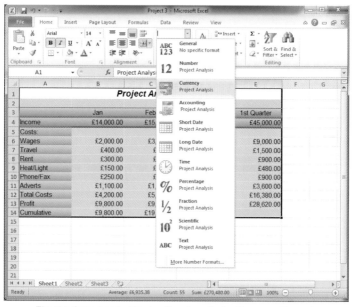

Fig. 5.5 Selecting to Display Numbers in the Currency Format

Above you also see what the result of your selection would be, as you hover the mouse pointer over the menu entries.

When you are satisfied that all is as it should be, click the **Save** button on the Quick Access Toolbar to save your work under the current filename. However, if you are not sure, and want to check later, then you could always use the **Save As** button and give your work a temporary filename (such as **Project 3a**) until you verify that your worksheet is identical to ours. When that is done, use the **File**, **Info** option, examine the contents of the displayed screen, then click the **Open File Location** button, which will allow you to rename your temporary file from a right-click menu. Try it!

Page Setup

Before printing a worksheet you should check and, if necessary, change the print settings. Most of the commands for this are in the **Page Layout**, **Page Setup** group shown here in Fig. 5.6.

Fig. 5.6 The Page Setup Group

Next, open **Project 3**, unless already opened, and click the Dialogue Box Launcher 🔲 to display the Page Setup screen shown in Fig. 5.7, with the Page tab open.

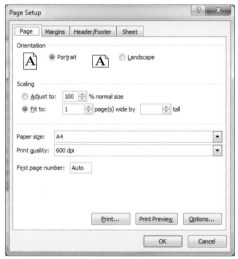

Fig. 5.7 Adjusting Page Settings

A very useful feature of Excel is the **Scaling** facility shown in the above dialogue box. You can print actual size or a percentage of it, or you can choose to fit your worksheet on to one page which allows Excel to scale your work automatically. We set the **Adjust to % normal size** to 130.

In the **Margins** tab we set the **Center on page** setting to **Horizontally** and clicked the Header/Footer tab to display Fig.5.8.

Fig. 5.8 The Header/Footer Tab Settings

Header and Footer Icons and Codes

Clicking the **Custom Header** button opens the Header box shown in Fig. 5.9 on the next page.

You can type text into any of the three boxes, or click on one of the buttons. **Sheet Name**, for example, inserts the **&[Tab]** code which has the effect of inserting the sheet name of the current active sheet at the time of printing. The first icon button displays the Font dialogue box, while others display the following codes:

Code	Action
&[Page]	Inserts a page number.
&[Pages]	Inserts the total number of pages.
&[Date]	Inserts the current date.
&[Time]	Inserts the current time.
&[File]	Inserts the filename of the current workbook.

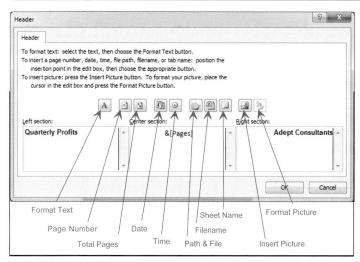

Fig. 5.9 Customising a Header

On the **Left** and **Right** sections we clicked the **Format Text** button and typed the displayed text in Arial 10 bold, while on the **Center section** we clicked the **Insert Page Number** button. Clicking **OK** returns you to the Page Setup screen, and clicking the **Print Preview** button, displays Fig. 5.10.

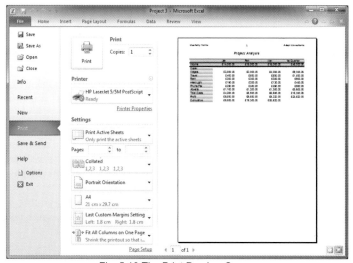

Fig. 5.10 The Print Preview Screen

Before pressing the **Print** button, check your work using the **View**, **Page Layout** command in the **Workbook Views** group, to display the screen in Fig. 5.11 below.

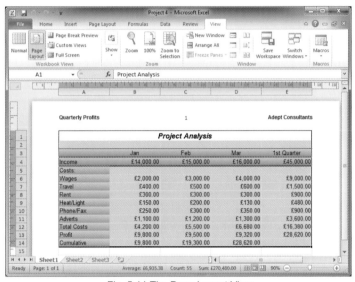

Fig. 5.11 The Page Layout View

When all is set, save your work as **Project 4**, then click the **File**, **Print** button to return to the screen in Fig. 5.10.

From this screen, you can choose your printer and its properties. Under **Settings** click the down-arrow against

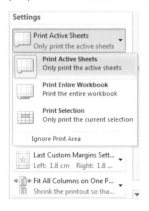

Print Active Sheets to display Fig. 5.12. As you can see, you can choose to print the **Active Sheets**, the **Entire Workbook**, or a **Selection**. If you have included headers and footers, these will be printed out irrespective of whether you choose to print a selected range or a selected worksheet. Clicking the **Print** button will start the printing operation.

Fig. 5.12 The Settings Options

3-Dimensional Worksheets

In Excel, a Workbook is a 3-dimensional file made up with a series of flat 2-dimensional sheets stacked 'on top of each other'. As mentioned previously, each separate sheet in a file has its own Tab identifier at the bottom of the screen. Ranges can be set to span several different sheets to build up 3-dimensional blocks of data. These blocks can then be manipulated, copied or moved to other locations in the file. A cell can reference any other cell in the file, no matter what sheet it is on, and an extended range of functions can be used to process these 3-dimensional ranges.

The best way to demonstrate a new idea is to work through an example – we will use the worksheet saved under **Project 4**. But first use the **View**, **Normal** command buttons before proceeding with the copying.

Copying Sheets in a Workbook

We will now fill another three sheets behind the present one, in order to include information about ADEPT Consultants' trading during the other three quarters of the year. The easiest way of doing this is by copying the information in Sheet1, including the formatting and the entered formulae, onto the other three sheets, then edit the numerical information in these appropriately.

To simplify this operation, Excel has a facility which allows you to copy a sheet into a workbook. There are two ways of doing this: (a) with the mouse, or (b) from the Ribbon. With the mouse (being the easiest method), make the sheet you want to copy the current sheet, then press the **Ctrl** key, and while keeping it pressed, point with the mouse on the Tab of Sheet1 and drag it to the right, as shown in Fig. 5.13.

Fig. 5.13 Drag Copying a Sheet into a Workbook

A small black triangle indicates the place where the copy will be inserted, as shown above.

If you insert a copy, say before Sheet2, when you release the mouse button the inserted sheet will be given the name Sheet1(2), while inserting a second copy before Sheet2 will be given the name Sheet1(3). To delete a worksheet, right-click its tab and select **Delete** from the pop-up menu.

With the above method you retain not only the formatting, but also the width of the columns. If you try copying a worksheet to the clipboard, then pasting in onto another sheet, you will lose the column widths, but retain other formatting.

When you have three copies placed on your workbook, double-click the Tabs of Sheet1 and the three new sheets and change their names to 'Quarter 1', 'Quarter 2', etc., then change the formatting of cells E5:E14, as well as those of B12:D14, of all the worksheets, so they stand out from the rest, as shown in Fig. 5.14. We use the **Home**, **Format Cells** commands, then the **Border** & **Fill** tabs of the Format Cells dialogue box. We leave it to you to experiment with this.

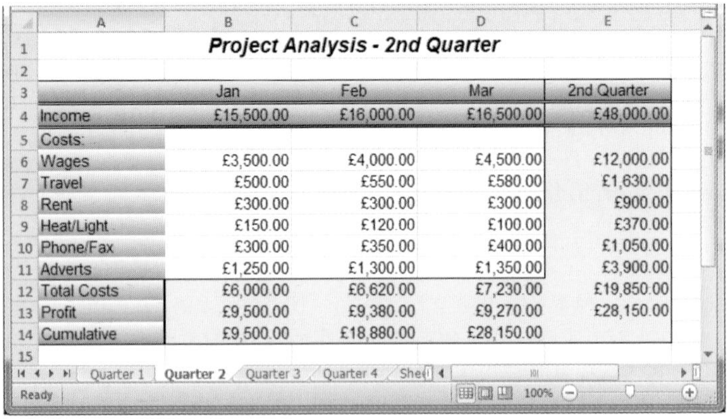

	A	B	C	D	E
1		Project Analysis - 2nd Quarter			
2					
3		Jan	Feb	Mar	2nd Quarter
4	Income	£15,500.00	£16,000.00	£16,500.00	£48,000.00
5	Costs:				
6	Wages	£3,500.00	£4,000.00	£4,500.00	£12,000.00
7	Travel	£500.00	£550.00	£580.00	£1,630.00
8	Rent	£300.00	£300.00	£300.00	£900.00
9	Heat/Light	£150.00	£120.00	£100.00	£370.00
10	Phone/Fax	£300.00	£350.00	£400.00	£1,050.00
11	Adverts	£1,250.00	£1,300.00	£1,350.00	£3,900.00
12	Total Costs	£6,000.00	£6,620.00	£7,230.00	£19,850.00
13	Profit	£9,500.00	£9,380.00	£9,270.00	£28,150.00
14	Cumulative	£9,500.00	£18,880.00	£28,150.00	
15					

Quarter 1 **Quarter 2** Quarter 3 Quarter 4 She
Ready   100%

Fig. 5.14 The Data for the Second Quarter

The correct contents of the second sheet should be as shown above. Be extra careful, from now on, to check the identification Tab at the bottom of the window, so as not to get the sheets mixed up. You don't want to spend time editing the wrong worksheet!

Next, build two additional sheets for the last two quarters of the year (see below for details on the 3rd and 4th quarters).

	Jul	Aug	Sep	Oct	Nov	Dec
Income	17,000	17,500	18,000	18,500	19,000	19,500
Costs:						
Wages	4,000	4,500	5,000	4,500	5,000	5,500
Travel	600	650	680	630	670	700
Rent	300	300	300	300	300	300
Heat/Light	50	80	120	160	200	250
Phone/Fax	350	380	420	400	420	450
Adverts	1,400	1,450	1,500	1,480	1,500	1,530

After building up the four worksheets (one for each quarter), save the file as **Project 5**.

Linking Sheets

Use the **Home**, **Cells**, **Insert** command and click **Insert Sheet** to place a worksheet in front of the 'stack' of data sheets to show a full year's results. Next, make a copy of the 1st Quarter sheet (using the **Home**, **Copy** button), and place it in the new front sheet (using the **Home**, **Paste** button). Note that column widths are not retained with this method, therefore you'll have to adjust these. Next, highlight cells B3 to E14, and press the **Delete** keyboard key and finally, rename the worksheet's Tab to 'Summary'.

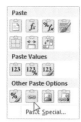

Fig. 5.15
Pasting Linked
Cells

We will now link the summary sheet to the other quarterly data sheets so that the information contained on them is automatically summarised and updated on it. The quarter totals in each Quarter's worksheet (cells E3 to E14) are selected and copied in turn using the **Home**, **Clipboard**, **Copy** button, and then pasted to the appropriate column of the summary sheet by selecting the destination range, and clicking the **Paste** button down-arrow and clicking the **Paste Link** icon pointed to in Fig. 5.15.

Do note that empty cells linked with this method, like those in cell E5 of each quarter, appear as 0 (zero) in the Summary sheet. These can be removed with the **Delete** key.

Next, insert appropriate formulae in row 14 to correctly calculate the cumulative values in the Summary sheet. The result should be as shown in Fig. 5.16 with the **Totals** shown in column F. Save the resultant workbook as **Project 6**.

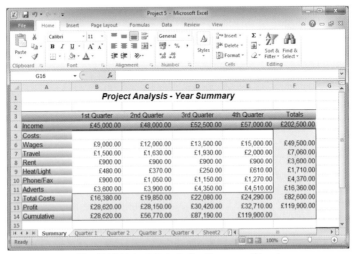

Fig. 5.16 Linked Data in the Summary Sheet

Relative and Absolute Cell Addresses

Entering a mathematical expression into Excel, such as the formula in cell C14 which was

=B14+C13

causes Excel to interpret it as 'add the contents of cell one column to the left of the current position, to the contents of cell one row above the current position'. In this way, when the formula was later copied into cell address D14, the contents of the cell relative to the left position of D14 (i.e. C14) and the contents of the cell one row above it (i.e. D13) were used, instead of the original cell addresses entered in C14. This is relative addressing.

To see the effect of relative versus absolute addressing, copy the formula in cell C14 into C16 using the **Copy** and **Paste** buttons, as shown in Fig. 5.17.

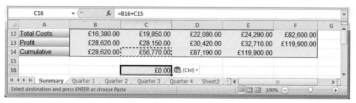

	C16			f_x	=B16+C15		
	A	B	C	D	E	F	G
12	Total Costs	£16,380.00	£19,850.00	£22,080.00	£24,290.00	£82,600.00	
13	Profit	£28,620.00	£28,150.00	£30,420.00	£32,710.00	£119,900.00	
14	Cumulative	£28,620.00	£56,770.00	£87,190.00	£119,900.00		
15							
16			£0.00	(Ctrl) ▾			

H ◀ ▶ H   Summary Quarter 1   Quarter 2   Quarter 3   Quarter 4   Sheet2

Select destination and press ENTER or choose Paste   100%

Fig. 5.17 Demonstrating Relative and Absolute Cell Addressing

Note that in cell C14 the formula was =B14+C13. However, when copied into cell C16 the formula appears as

=B16+C15

This is because it has been interpreted as relative addressing. In this case, no value appears in cell C16 because we are attempting to add two blank cells.

Now change the formula in cell C14 by editing it to

=$B$14+$C$13

which is interpreted as absolute addressing. Copying this formula into cell C16 calculates the correct result. Highlight cell C16 and observe the cell references in its formula; they have not changed from those of cell C14.

When creating a financial model in a spreadsheet it is common practice to put all the control parameters on a sheet of their own. These might be the $/£ exchange rate, or the % rate of inflation for example. Whenever these parameters are needed in a cell formula in the model they should not just be entered straight into the formula, but absolute references should be made to them in the parameter sheet. In this way you can change a parameter in one place on the parameter sheet and see the overall effects when the model is recalculated. The $ sign must prefix both the column reference and the row reference.

Mixed cell addressing is permitted; as for example when a column address reference is needed to be taken as absolute, while a row address reference is not.

Freezing Panes on Screen

With large sheets when you are working in the data area you may not be able to see the label cells associated with that data and it is easy to get very confused.

To get over this you can freeze column (or row) labels of a worksheet on screen so that they are always visible. To do this, move the cell pointer to the right (or below) the column (or row) which you want to freeze, and click the **View**, **Window**, **Freeze Panes** command button shown in Fig. 5.18. Selecting **Freeze Panes** from the drop-down menu will place black lines in the sheet to show what is frozen. Then everything to the left of, or above the cell pointer will freeze on the screen when you scroll through the worksheet.

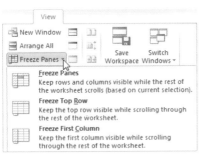

Fig. 5.18 The Freeze Panes Button

To unfreeze panes, click the **View**, **Window**, **Freeze Panes** button again and select the **Unfreeze Panes** option. This is only available if you have rows or columns frozen.

In Excel 2010 you cannot use Page Layout view with frozen panes in your sheet. The warning message shown below opens. If you click the **OK** button, the sheet will be unfrozen.

Fig. 5.19 Another Excel Warning Message

Spreadsheet Charts

Excel 2010 makes it very easy to create professional looking charts or graphs from your data. The saying 'a picture is worth a thousand words', applies equally well to charts and figures. They allow you to visually see data trends and patterns.

As we shall see, the package can almost instantly create many different chart and graph types, including area, bar, column, line, doughnut, radar, XY, pie, combination and several 3-D options of these charts. These are made available to you once you have selected the data you want to chart from the **Charts** group on the **Insert** tab.

Charts (you can have several per worksheet) can be displayed on screen at the same time as the worksheet from which they were derived, since they are created in their own chart frame and can be embedded anywhere on a worksheet. They can be sent to an appropriate output device, such as a plotter or printer, or copied to another program such as Word or PowerPoint.

A Simple Column Chart

To illustrate some of the graphing capabilities of Excel, we will plot the income of the consulting company we discussed in the **Project 6** file. If you haven't already done so, you will need to complete the exercise described earlier (see pages 108 & 109) and have to hand the linked workbook shown in Fig. 5.16 on page 110.

Now we need to select the range of the data we want to graph. The range of data to be graphed in Excel does not have to be contiguous for each graph, as with some other spreadsheets. With Excel, you select your data from different parts of a sheet with the **Ctrl** key pressed down. This method has the advantage of automatic recalculation should any changes be made to the original data. You could also collect data from different sheets to one 'graphing' sheet by linking them as we did with the summary sheet.

If you don't want the chart to be recalculated when you do this, then you must use the **Home**, **Clipboard**, **Copy** and **Paste**, **Paste Special** command buttons and choose the **Values** option from the displayed dialogue box. This copies a selected range to a specified target area of the worksheet and converts formulas to values. This is necessary, as cells containing formulas cannot be pasted directly since it would cause the relative cell addresses to adjust to the new locations; each formula would then recalculate a new value for each cell and give wrong results.

Creating a Chart

To obtain a chart of 'Income' versus 'Quarters', select the data in cell range A3..E4, then click the **Insert**, **Charts**, **Column** button, shown below in Fig. 5.20.

Fig. 5.20 Charting Buttons on the Insert Tab

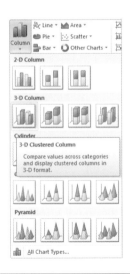

This opens the drop-down gallery of chart options shown in Fig. 5.21. Now select the **3-D Clustered Column** type and just click it to create the chart shown in Fig. 5.22 on the next page. That's all there is to it, just a few clicks!

Fig. 5.21 The Column Charts Gallery

Fig. 5.22 A 3-D Clustered Column Chart

While the frame containing a chart is selected (you can tell from the presence of the handles around it), you can change its size by dragging the small two-headed arrow pointer (which appears when the mouse pointer is placed on the handles at the corners or middle of the frame). You can also move the frame and its contents to another position on the worksheet by dragging it to a new position.

The Chart Tools

When you select a chart in Excel by clicking it, the **Chart Tools** add the **Design**, **Layout**, and **Format** tabs, as below.

Fig. 5.23 The Design Tab of the Charting Ribbon

The Design tab groups controls for you to change the chart Type, Data, Chart Layouts, Chart Styles and Location.

Fig. 5.24 The Layout Tab of the Charting Ribbon

With this tab you control the layout of the Current Selection, Labels, and Axes, Insert a layout, and Background, Analysis and Properties.

Fig. 5.25 The Format Tab of the Charting Ribbon

From the Format tab you format the Current Selection, set Shape Styles and WordArt Styles, Arrange objects and Size.

Customising a Chart

Now it is time for you to 'play'. The only way to find out what all the charting controls do is to try them all out. Remember that some options are applied to the chart element that is currently selected, others to the whole chart.

Fig. 5.26 The Chart Elements Box

To control what is selected, click the arrow next to the **Chart Elements** box (below the **File** command button) in the **Current Selection** group of the **Format** tab, and then click the chart element that you want, as shown in Fig. 5.26.

On the **Layout** tab, we suggest you click the label layout option that you want in the **Labels** group, select what chart axes you want in the **Axes** group, and what layout option you want in the **Background** group.

In the **Current Selection** group, clicking **Format Selection**, opens a Format control box like that shown in Fig. 5.27 on the next page, in which you select the formatting options you want for the selected chart element.

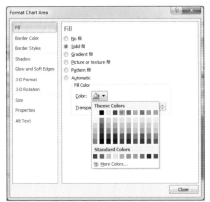

Fig. 5.27 Setting Format Options for Chart Elements

You can also apply a quick style to individual elements, or use the **Shape Fill**, **Shape Outline**, and **Shape Effects** buttons in the **Shape Quick Styles** group on the **Format** tab. These are our favourite ways of formatting our charts.

Try it, then change the May income (on the Quarter 2 sheet) from £16,000 to £26,000, and watch how the change is reflected on the redrawn graph. Finally, revert to the original entry for the May income, and if you like, change your chart back to its original column type, and then save your work again under the filename **Project 7** by clicking the **Save** button on the Quick Access toolbar. Your current work will be saved to disc replacing the previous version.

When Excel creates a chart, it plots each row or column of data in the selected range as a 'data series', such as a group of bars, lines, etc. A chart can contain many data series, but Excel charts data according to the following rules:

1.   If the selected range contains more rows than columns of data, Excel plots the data series by columns.

2.   If the selected range contains more columns than rows of data, or the same number of columns and rows, Excel plots the data series by rows.

If you select a range to chart which includes column and row headings, and text above or to the left of the numeric data, Excel uses the text to create the axis labels, legends, and title.

Saving Charts

When you save a workbook, the chart or charts you have created are saved with it. It is, therefore, a good idea not only to give each chart a title (select it then use the **Chart Tools**, **Layout** tab, **Properties**, and rename **Chart 1** to **Income Column** and press **Enter**).

It is also a good idea to locate charts on a separate sheet. To do this, click the Insert Worksheet 🔲 tab at the bottom of the screen, move the new sheet in front of the Summary tab and rename it Charts. Use **Cut** and **Paste** to move the chart from its present position to the Charts tab sheet, and save the workbook as **Project 7**.

Predefined Chart Types

To select a different type of chart, click the **Design**, **Type**, **Change Chart Type** button shown here. Excel 2010 uses 11 basic chart types, and with variations of these has 73 type options in all. These chart-types are normally used to describe the following relationships between data:

for showing a volume relationship between two series, such as production or sales, over a given length of time.

for comparing differences in data (noncontinuous data that are not related over time) by depicting changes in horizontal bars to show positive and negative variations from a given position.

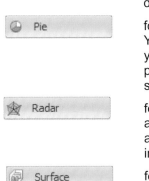

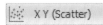

for showing a type of XY (scatter) chart. The size of the data (radius of the bubble) indicates the value of a third variable.

for comparing separate items (noncontinuous data which are related over time) by depicting changes in vertical bars to show positive and negative variations from a given position.

for comparing parts with the whole. Similar to pie charts, but can depict more than one series of data.

for showing continuous changes in data with time.

for comparing parts with the whole. You can use this type of chart when you want to compare the percentage of an item from a single series of data with the whole series.

for plotting one series of data as angle values defined in radians, against one or more series defined in terms of a radius.

for showing optimum combinations between two sets of data, as in a topographic map. Colours and patterns indicate areas that are in the same range of values.

for showing high-low-close type of data variation to illustrate stock market prices or temperature changes.

for showing scatter relationships between X and Y. Scatter charts are used to depict items which are not related over time.

Drawing a Multiple Column Chart

As an exercise, we will consider a new column chart which deals with the quarterly 'Costs' of Adept Consultants. To achieve this, first select the Summary sheet of workbook **Project 7**, then highlight the cell range A3:E3, press the **Ctrl** key, and holding it down, use the mouse to select the costs range A6:E11.

Next, click the **Insert**, **Charts**, **Column** button, select Clustered Cylinder from the gallery as pointed to below. The 6 different quarterly costs will be drawn automatically, as displayed in the composite 'before and after' screen dump in Fig. 5.28.

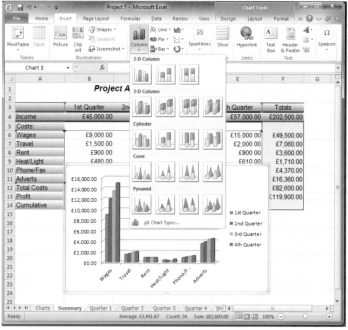

Fig. 5.28 Creating a Costs Column Chart

Because the selected range contains more rows than columns of data, Excel follows the 1st rule of data series selection, which is not really what we want.

To have the 'quarters' appearing on the x-axis and the 'costs' as the legends, we need to tell Excel that our data series is in rows by clicking the **Design**, **Data**, **Switch Row/Column** button on the Ribbon. Immediately this is done the column chart changes to:

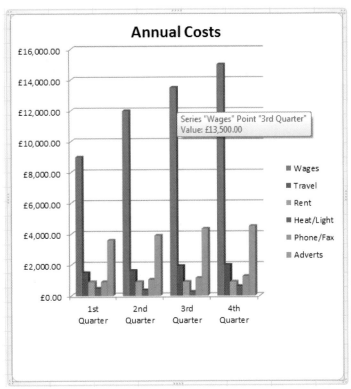

Fig. 5.29 The Costs Column Chart on its own Sheet

The chart title was added by clicking the **Layout**, **Labels**, **Chart Title** button, selecting **Above Chart** and then typing the heading in the object space provided on the chart.

Finally we moved the chart to the Chart Tab sheet, as before, and renamed it **Costs Column** using the **Chart Tools**, **Layout** tab, **Properties** command buttons. Save the workbook under its existing name by clicking the **Save** button on the Quick Access toolbar.

Changing Titles and Labels

To change a title, an axis label or a legend within a chart, click the appropriate area on the chart. This reveals that these are individual objects (they are surrounded by small green circles and squares called 'handles') and you can edit, reposition, or change their font and point size. You can even rotate text within such areas in any direction you like.

To demonstrate some of these options, we will use the **Costs Column** chart saved in **Project 7**, so get it on screen if you are to follow our suggestions.

To change the font size of a chart title, click in the Chart Title area to select it and select the existing title text. Then simply click the **Home** tab and use any of the **Font** group buttons. Below, in Fig. 5.30, we show what happens when you select to change the colour of the chart title by clicking on the **Font Color** button.

You can also change the colour of the chart title by using the options on the **Format**, **WordArt Styles** group and clicking the **Text Fill** button. Either way can make your chart or axis titles really stand out. There are also options to apply a gradient or a texture to a title.

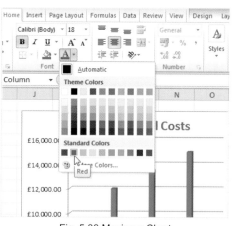

Fig. 5.30 Moving a Chart

The **WordArt Styles** group also has the **Text Outline** and **Text Effects** buttons, which include Shadow, Reflection and Glow effects. The possibilities are almost limitless!

Drawing a Pie Chart

Change Chart Type

To change the chart type, simply select the chart, click the **Design**, **Type**, **Change Chart Type** button, shown here, and choose from the gallery.

As a last example in chart drawing, we used the data ranges A6:A11 and F6:F11 of the Summary worksheet to plot an **Exploded Pie in 3-D** chart, as shown in Fig. 5.31 below.

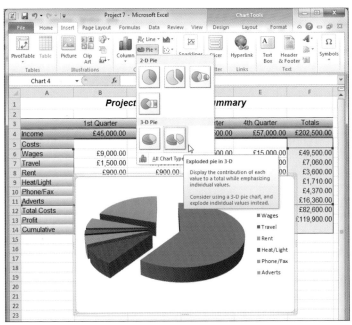

Fig. 5.31 A 3-D Pie Exploded Chart

Next, copy the chart to the Chart Tab of the workbook, and use the **Chart Tools**, **Layout**, **Labels**, **Data Labels** button and in the **More Data Label Options** section check the **Category name**, **Percentage** and **Show Leader Lines** check boxes. Then just drag things around and re-size them to obtain the pie chart shown in Fig. 5.32 on the next page. We chose to copy rather than move the chart from its original place, so that a copy of it is available in case of mistakes!

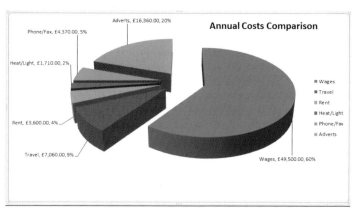

Fig. 5.32 The Final 3-D Pie Exploded Chart

This chart tells us, for example, that Wages for the whole year amount to 60% of the total yearly costs. Other cost categories are also displayed with their appropriate percentages. Pointing to any pie slice, opens a pop-up showing the actual data series, its value and its percentage of the whole.

Sparklines

New to Excel 2010 is the ability to examine trends in data by providing a tiny chart representation of the data in one cell. In this way, you can see at a glance the trend in the underlying data.

To illustrate how you can use sparklines, we copied the **Heat/Light** costs from each quarter and pasted them into the Summary sheet of our **Project 7** workbook, as shown in Fig. 5.33 on the next page. To make it easy to show you what we are doing, we copied the data from each quarter, but pasted them into two six-monthly rows.

Next, select the range of the first six-monthly data (A19 to F19) and click the **Insert**, **Sparklines**, **Lines** button. This opens the Create Sparklines dialogue box in which the **Data Range** is already inserted, but you need to provide the **Location Range** which in this case is G19.

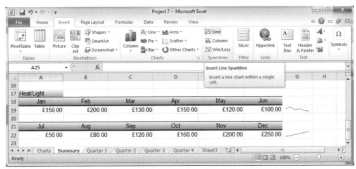

Fig. 5.33 Illustrating Sparklines

Obviously this example is rather too feeble, but it is the technique that matters.

Excel Web App

Just as with Word Web App, Excel Web App is part of Microsoft Web Apps which allows you to create Word, Excel, PowerPoint and OneNote documents on Windows Live. This allows you to work with documents directly on the Web site where they are stored.

To use this facility, as we mentioned in the case of Word, you must set up a Windows Live ID, which is very easy to do and is free! If you already use Hotmail, Messenger, or Xbox Live, then you already have a Windows Live ID. If not, do the following:

Use your Internet Explorer and go to the www.live.com Web site. In the displayed screen, click the **Sign up** link and fill in the required information, then click the **I accept** button. It is as easy as that!

You can now start using Excel Web App by saving your latest workbook (**Project 7**) to Windows Live SkyDrive. Use the **File**, **Save & Send** command button, then click **Save to Web**, and select **My Documents** (see Fig. 3.26 on page 67). You can also use the **File**, **Save & Send** command to publish an Excel workbook to a Blog site, send it as an attachment to an e-mail, or as a PDF.

To retrieve an Excel workbook from SkyDrive (from anywhere in the World), use your Internet Explorer and go to www.live.com, sign in with your Live ID and Password, click on **Office** and select **Your Documents**, then **My Documents**.

Now, by clicking the required workbook on SkyDrive, it is loaded into Excel Web App, as shown in Fig. 5.34, and then you can use the **File** command button to display a menu of options, such as Open in Excel, Print, Share, etc.

Fig. 5.34 Loading a Workbook into Excel Web App for Viewing or Printing

Clicking the **Edit in Browser** button in Fig. 5.34 above, opens the Excel Web App and loads your workbook as shown in Fig. 5.35. As you can see, although the options available on the Ribbon are a limited version to those in Excel, they are quite adequate. We leave it to you to explore.

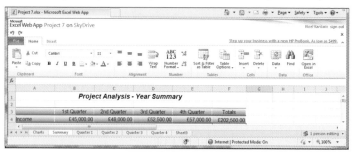

Fig. 5.35 Loading a Document into Excel Web App for Editing

* * *

Excel 2010 has many more features than the ones we have introduced here. For example, you could use Excel's database and macro capabilities, and also explore its various tools, such as the Goal Seek, Scenarios, Auditing, and Solver. We hope we have given you sufficient basic knowledge to be able to explore these topics by yourself.

6

The PowerPoint Environment

PowerPoint 2010

Microsoft PowerPoint provides an easy way to quickly generate powerful, attractive presentations or slide shows, using text, graphics, the SmartArt graphics, advanced slide layout capabilities and style galleries. With PowerPoint, you can save time creating and formatting presentations with Themes that give a consistent look and feel across all your Office 2010 documents.

PowerPoint 2010, just as its predecessor PowerPoint 2007, takes advantage of the Ribbon interface, and includes several other improvements over earlier versions of the program, such as:

- Using SmartArt graphics to create professional visual illustrations of your ideas which are fully editable.

- Create custom layouts containing as many place holders as you need for charts, tables, movies, pictures, SmartArt graphics, clip art and text.

- Add effects like shadow, reflection, glow, soft edges, warp, bevel, 3-D rotation to shapes, SmartArt graphics, tables, text and WordArt.

- Use of themes, layouts and Quick Styles that offer a wide range of formatting options.

In addition, PowerPoint 2010 introduces several new tools and features that can be used to effectively create and manage presentations, and use them to collaborate with other colleagues or co-authors. For example, amongst the many new features, you can now do the following:

- Manage your PowerPoint files from the new Office Backstage view.

- Organise your slides into sections and access them from anywhere in the world by using the PowerPoint Web App.

- Add video, pictures, animation, and make your presentation portable and even turn them easily into a video or slide show.

- Co-author a presentation easily with others by being allowed to change a shared presentation at the same time rather than separately.

Starting PowerPoint

To start PowerPoint 2010, use the **Start**, **All Programs** command, select the **Microsoft Office** entry from the displayed menu, and click **Microsoft PowerPoint 2010**, as shown in Fig. 6.1.

Fig. 6.1 Using the Start Menu

You can also double-click on a PowerPoint file in a Windows folder, in which case the presentation will be loaded into PowerPoint at the same time.

The PowerPoint Window

When PowerPoint is loaded, a screen displays with a similar **File** button, Quick Access toolbar, Title bar and Ribbon to those of Word and Excel. Obviously there are differences, but that is to be expected as PowerPoint serves a different purpose to the other programs.

The opening presentation screen of PowerPoint is shown in Fig. 6.2 below. The program follows the usual Microsoft Windows conventions with which you should be very familiar by now. Scroll bars and scroll buttons only appear when you have more than one slide in your presentation.

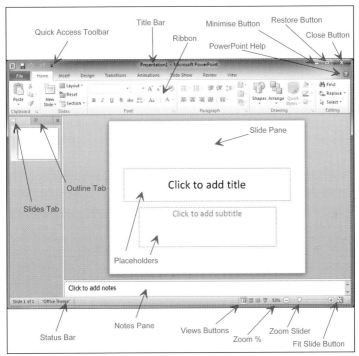

Fig. 6.2 Parts of the Default PowerPoint Opening Screen

The Ribbon

The PowerPoint 2010 Ribbon has eight tabs, each one with the most used controls grouped on it for the main program actions. For a general description of the Ribbon, see page 5.

Fig. 6.3 The Home Tab of the PowerPoint 2010 Ribbon

A quick look at the Home tab, shown in Fig. 6.3, shows that it contains groups for the more common PowerPoint activities. The Clipboard cut and paste commands, add Slides, format text Font and Paragraph, work with Drawing Shapes, Quick Styles, and arrange your work, and ability for Editing text.

Clicking a new tab opens a new series of groups, each with its relevant command buttons. The contents of the other tabs allow you to do the following:

• The Insert tab enables you to immediately insert Tables, Images, Illustrations (such as Shapes, SmartArt and Charts), Links, Text based features, Symbols and Media Clips (such as Video and Audio).

• The Design tab groups controls for Page Setup, choosing and modifying Themes and controlling the Background of your slides.

• The Transitions tab allows you to add, control the Timing and Preview your work.

• The Animations tab allows you to add Animation and control its Timing.

• The Slide Show tab groups the actions used when Starting a Slide Show, Setting it Up and controlling your Monitors.

• The Review tab gives you control for Proofing your presentation and to initiate and track review and approval processes. It lets you add, edit, delete and move between Comments.

• The View tab is where you go to set what you see on the screen. You can choose between Presentation Views, Master Views, Show or Hide screen features, Zoom to different magnifications, change between Color and Grayscale, control Windows and run and record Macros.

It is worth spending some time here examining the various Ribbon tabs and the commands grouped within them. You could also use Help (see next section) to find out more specific details.

Help in PowerPoint

Whether you have used a previous version of PowerPoint or not, the first time you use the program, it might be a good  idea to click the **Microsoft Office PowerPoint Help** button on the Ribbon, or press the **F1** keyboard key. These open the Help window shown in Fig. 6.4.

Now, clicking the **Show Table of Contents** button (pointed to in Fig. 6.4), displays Fig. 6.5 in which a list of available help topics in the form of closed books appear on the left pane. Left-clicking one of these books opens it and displays a further list of topics with icons. Clicking any of these opens the relevant Help page in the right-hand pane.

Fig. 6.4 The PowerPoint Help Window

Fig. 6.5

After looking at 'What's new', have a look at the other options in the **Table of Contents** list. We suggest you spend a little time here browsing through the various topics before going on. To get more help from the Office Online Web site, you can click on the links at the right pane of the Help page.

PowerPoint Templates

Before we can look at the views of PowerPoint's main working area, we need to have a presentation active in the program. If you have a saved presentation, you can click the **File** ▦ command button and select the **Open** option on the Backstage screen, shown here in Fig. 6.6.

If not, press the **New** button to open the Available Templates and Themes list, part of which is shown in Fig. 6.7. This lists all the **Templates** that are available to you for creating new presentations, including a large number to be found online.

Fig. 6.6 Part of Office

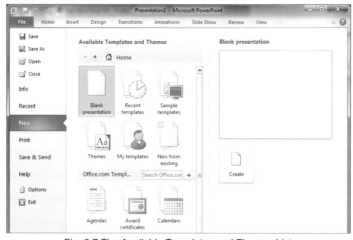

Fig. 6.7 The Available Templates and Themes List

There are six sources of templates and themes installed on your computer for you to choose from:

Blank presentation – opens a slide with no formatting at all.

Recent templates – opens any recently used templates.

Sample templates – opens several pre-installed templates.

Themes – lists various themes.

My templates – lists templates you saved yourself.

New from existing – lets you create a new presentation from an existing one saved on your PC.

It is worth spending some time looking at what is available here. Some templates, including those found online contain a full presentation for you to use and practise with. Having examined a template, to get back to the **Available Templates and Themes**, click the **Home** button or the **File** **New** command buttons.

For now, open the **Sample Templates**, shown in Fig. 6.7, by double-clicking its icon, scroll down a little way, then locate and double-click the **Introducing PowerPoint 2010** icon, shown in Fig. 6.8, to open the 20 slide presentation screen shown in Fig. 6.9 on the next page. Yours may be different depending on your Office 2010 installation.

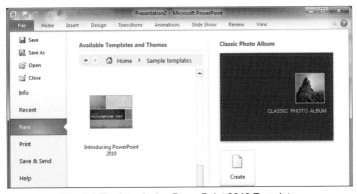

Fig. 6.8 The Introducing PowerPoint 2010 Template

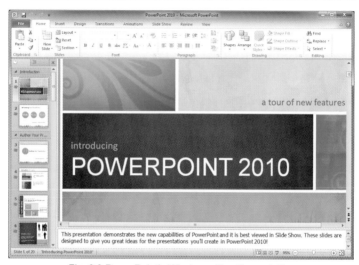

Fig. 6.9 PowerPoint's Window with a Presentation

We actually saved the above as a presentation by clicking the **File** ‌ command button and selecting the **Save As** option on the Backstage screen. In this way, whatever we do to this presentation, we still have the original intact.

PowerPoint by default shows a presentation in Normal View. If you are following this on your PC, have a look through this presentation. Both the main panes now have vertical scroll bars which you can use to move through the individual slides, but the current slide will always show completely and be re-scaled if you re-size the program window. The two arrow buttons below the right-hand scroll bar let you step up ▲ or down ▼ through the slides.

In PowerPoint Microsoft uses the word slide to refer to each individual page of a presentation and you can format the output for overhead projector acetates, or for electronic presentation on screen.

PowerPoint Views

You need to change your working view often in PowerPoint so they have made it easy to do, from the Ribbon in the **View**, **Presentation Views** group of controls. For **Normal**, **Slide Sorter** and **Reading View** the controls are also on the Status Bar toolbar. Also on the Status Bar you will find the **Slide Show** control button (which also appears on the **Slide Show** tab on the Ribbon), and an additional button that refits the slide to the window after zooming operations.

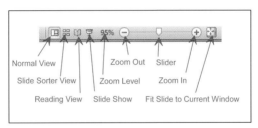

Fig. 6.10 The Views Control Toolbar

Normal View

The Normal view is the main editing view, which is used to write and design a presentation. The view has four working areas: on the left, two tabs alternate between an Outline view of your slide text and a Slide view (thumbnails display of your slides); on the right, the slide pane displays a large view of the current slide; and on the bottom, the Notes pane.

You can use these panes to work on all aspects of your presentation, and you can adjust their size by dragging their borders. The Slides and Outline tabs change to display an icon when the pane becomes narrow, and if you only want to see the current slide in the window as you edit, you can close the pane with the ⊠ **Close** button, shown in Fig. 6.11.

The Slides tab, shown on the left in Fig. 6.11 on the next page, shows the slides in your presentation as thumbnails. They make it easy for you to navigate through your presentation and to see the effects of any design changes. You can also easily rearrange, add or delete slides here.

The Outline tab, shown on the right in Fig. 6.11 below, shows your slide text in outline form. This is a good place to enter and edit the text of your presentation.

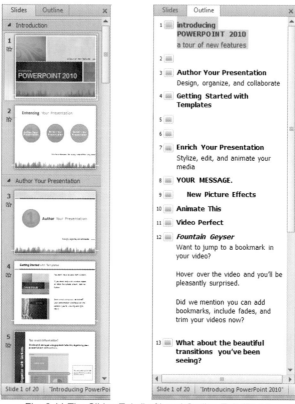

Fig. 6.11 The Slides Tab (Left) and Outline Tab (Right)

The Slide pane displays a large and zoomable view of the current slide. You can add text and insert pictures, tables, SmartArt graphics, charts, drawing objects, text boxes, movies, sounds, hyperlinks and animations.

The Notes pane, below the Slide pane, is used to type notes that apply to the current slide. Later, you can print your notes and refer to them when you give your presentation or give them as handouts to your audience.

Notes Page View

If you want to view and work with your slide notes in full-page mode you can use the Notes Page view, opened by clicking the **View**, **Presentation Views**, **Notes Page** button.

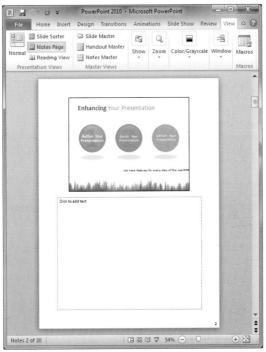

Fig. 6.12 Notes Page View

As shown in Fig. 6.12, the Notes Page view has two panes. The upper one showing the current slide, and the lower one to hold your notes. You can add pictures here as well.

Slide Show View

Slide Show view takes up the full computer screen, like an actual presentation. In this view, you see your presentation the way an audience will. You can see how your graphics, timings, movies, animated effects and transition effects will look during the actual presentation.

To see the next slide in full-screen view, either click the left mouse button or press the right arrow key. To return to a previous slide in full-screen view press the left arrow key. To return to a previous PowerPoint view from a full-screen view, press **Esc**, or click the right mouse button to display the menu shown in Fig. 6.13, and click **End Show**.

Fig. 6.13 Right-click Menu

Slide Sorter View

In this view (Fig. 6.14), you can see the whole presentation at once. You can reorder slides, add transitions and set timing for electronic presentations. You can also select animated transitions for moving from slide to slide.

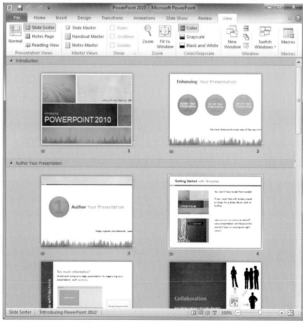

Fig. 6.14 The Slide Sorter View

Setting Animations

Your presentation will appear more professional if you set animations and transitions. To provide additional emphasis, or show your information in phases, you can animate or add special visual or sound effects to text or objects in your presentation. For example, you could apply a fly-in animation to all items on a slide or apply the animation to a single paragraph in a bulleted list.

To do this, click the text or object that you want to animate (we chose the third ball of the second slide in order to illustrate the process), and on the **Animations** tab, in the **Animations** group, select the animation effect that you want from the **Animation Styles** list shown in Fig. 6.15 (we chose the **Bounce** effect). Check the effect by clicking the **Preview** button.

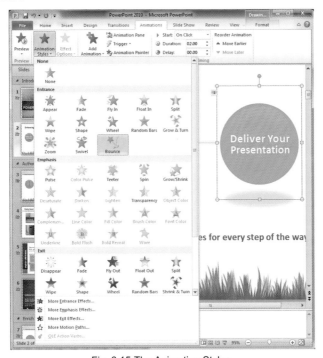

Fig. 6.15 The Animation Styles

Adding Transitions

Slide transitions are animation-like effects that occur in **Slide Show** view when the show moves from one slide to the next. You can control the speed of each slide transition effect, and you can also add sound.

In **Normal** view select a slide and click the **Transitions** tab, then in the **Transition To This Slide** group, select any of the available slide transitions, such as **Shred**, **Switch**, **Flip**, or click the **Gallery** button, active in Fig. 6.16 below, to see a lot more effects. Your slide in the Slides Pane will demonstrate the effects as you move between them. To set the slide transition speed click the down-arrow next to the **Duration** button, and select the speed that you want.

When you are happy with your choice click the **Apply to All** command button.

Fig. 6.16 Adding a Transition

In the next Chapter we will try to design a presentation from scratch, so that you can apply some of the skills you have gained so far.

7

Designing a Presentation

In this chapter we will use some of PowerPoint's tools to design a simple presentation quickly and effectively. Below, we show the first page of the finished presentation so that you can have an idea of the overall design.

Fig. 7.1 The First Page of our Presentation

By default, when PowerPoint 2010 opens it applies the Blank Presentation template, and uses the Office Theme for new presentations. Blank Presentation is the simplest of the templates in PowerPoint. It is a good one to use when you first start, as it is plain and can be adapted to many presentation types.

To create a new presentation based on the Blank Presentation template, either restart PowerPoint, or click the **File** command button, then click **New**, and double-click **Blank Presentation**, under **Available Templates and Themes**, as shown in Fig. 6.7 on page 132.

Initial Setup

These days, most presentations are probably given electronically, either in person, by e-mail, or from a Web site, but the first thing to do is to check the initial page setup for your presentation.

To do this click the **Page Setup** button, shown here, located on the **Design** tab to open the Page Setup box shown below.

Fig. 7.2 The Page Setup Dialogue Box

In the **Slides sized for** drop-down list select from several on-screen sizes, your paper size if the presentation is to be printed on paper or acetate, 35 mm slides and others. If necessary, select **Portrait** or **Landscape** orientations.

Applying a Theme

PowerPoint 2010 provides a wide variety of design themes that make it easy to change the overall look of your presentation. As we have seen earlier, a theme is a set of design elements that provides a specific, unified appearance for all of your Office documents by using particular combinations of colours, fonts and effects.

PowerPoint automatically applies the Office theme to presentations that are created with the Blank Presentation template, but it is easy to change the look of your presentation at any time by applying a different theme. If you can choose your theme before you put data on your slides, you will save a lot of 'fiddly' work later though.

On the **Design** tab, in the **Themes** group, you can preview how your slide will look with a particular theme applied by hovering the pointer on a choice as shown below. To apply a theme, just click it.

Fig. 7.3 Selecting a Theme for the Presentation

We liked the Aspect theme, as shown above, but you can choose what you want.

By default, PowerPoint 2010 applies themes to the entire presentation. If you only want to change a few slides, select them on the Slides tab on the Slides Pane, right-click the theme that you want to apply to them, and then click **Apply to Selected Slides** on the context menu, as shown below.

If you decide later that you want a different theme, click that theme to apply it.

Fig. 7.4 Context Menu

Adding Text to a Slide

The single opening slide that is provided automatically in your presentation has two placeholders, one formatted for a title and the other formatted for a subtitle. This arrangement of placeholders on a slide is called a layout.

Click the placeholder where you want to add the text, and type in, or paste, the text that you want to add.

Fig. 7.5 Entering Text into a Placeholder

Here we have typed in the presentation title and it has been automatically formatted with the theme font features, while the subtitle awaits our attention.

Formatting Text

Hopefully the theme formatting will be fine, but if not you can apply any changes of your own to any text you enter. There are many ways to change the appearance of text on a slide, ranging from the basic buttons on the **Home** tab for formatting font, style, size, colour, alignment and other paragraph characteristics, to the **WordArt Styles** features on the **Format** tab.

Bulleted Lists

Some placeholders automatically format your text as a bulleted list, but you can control this. Clicking the **Home**, **Paragraph**, **Bullets** button will switch the text selected between a bulleted list and unbulleted text.

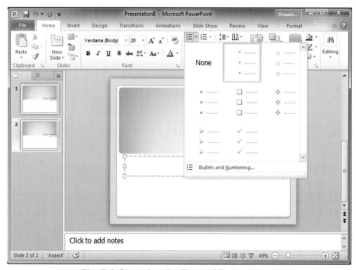

Fig. 7.6 Changing the Type of Bullets Used

To change the style of the bullet characters in a bulleted list, click the arrow next to **Bullets**, and then click the bullet style that you want, as in Fig. 7.6 above. You can also make these changes with the Mini toolbar.

Adding Slides

To add a slide to your presentation, you first choose a layout for the new slide, if it is to be different from your first slide, as described earlier. To do this, click the arrow next to the **Home**, **Slides**, **New Slide** button to open the gallery in Fig. 7.7, showing thumbnails of the various slide layouts that are available.

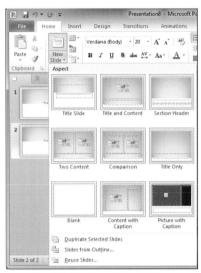

Fig. 7.7 The New Slide Gallery

There are layout options for most types of slides, most with placeholders. Those that display coloured icons can contain text, but you can also click an icon to automatically insert a table, chart, SmartArt graphic, picture from file, clip art or a media clip, as shown in Fig. 7.8 below.

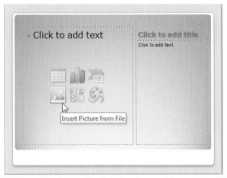

Fig. 7.8 The Content with Caption Layout for a New Slide

Click the layout that you want for your new slide and it will appear both on the Slides tab, and the Slide pane. If you want your new slide to have the same layout that the preceding slide has, you can just click the **New Slide** button.

Manipulating Slides

Fig. 7.9 Slide Context Menu

To copy a slide with its content and layout, right-click the slide that you want to copy on the Slides tab, and select **Copy** on the context menu, shown in Fig. 7.9. Then right-click in the Slides tab where you want to add the new copy, and select **Paste**. You can then make any changes you want to the new slide.

While you are in the Slides tab, you can drag slides up and down the list to rearrange them in the presentation. To delete a slide, right-click it in the Slides tab and select the **Delete Slide** option.

Adding Pictures

You can insert or copy pictures and clip art into a PowerPoint presentation from commercial suppliers, Web pages, or files on your computer. You can also use pictures and clip art as backgrounds for your slides.

Inserting a Picture from a File

Click where you want to insert the picture, either in a

Fig. 7.10 Selecting and Inserting a Picture into a Slide

placeholder, or on the slide itself, then click the **Insert**, **Images**, **Picture** command button.

Next, locate the picture you want to insert, and double-click it. The result of such an action is shown here in Fig. 7.10.

To add multiple pictures, press and hold the **Ctrl** key while you click the pictures that you want to insert, and then click the **Insert** button.

Pictures that you insert from a file are embedded in a presentation. You can reduce the size of a file by linking a picture instead. In the Insert Picture dialogue box, shown in Fig. 7.11 below, select the picture that you want to insert, click the arrow next to the **Insert** button, and then click **Link to File**.

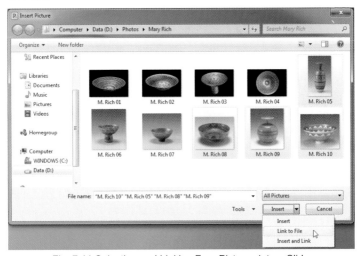

Fig. 7.11 Selecting and Linking Four Pictures into a Slide

To copy a picture from a Web page, right-click the picture and select **Copy** on the shortcut menu. In your presentation, right-click where you want to insert the picture, and click **Paste**.

If you don't select a placeholder for the picture, or if you select a placeholder that can't contain an image, the picture is inserted at the centre of the slide. You can now move it, re-size it, rotate it, add text to it, or even delete it from a right-click menu.

When you select a picture or other type of graphic in PowerPoint the **Picture Tools** become available in the **Format** tab as shown in Fig. 7.10 and Fig. 7.12.

The **Picture Tools** commands let you add effects to images such as a shadow, glow, crop, compress, re-size and remove image background. The latter does not always work for all of our images, perhaps because of image reflections.

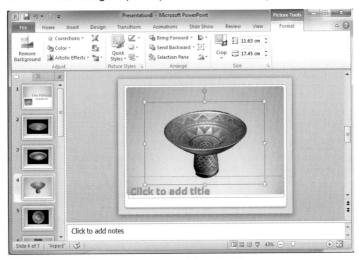

Fig. 7.12 Removing a Picture Background

To change the size of a picture, hold the pointer over one of the corner selection handles, as shown below, and drag the image to the size you want.

Fig. 7.13 The Resizing Operation

To move the picture, just drag it with the ✛ pointer to wherever you want on the slide.

Saving a Presentation

As with any software program, it is a good idea to name and save your presentation right away and to remember to save your changes frequently while you work. That way you won't lose your hard work. The quickest way to save a document to disc is to click the **Save** button on the Quick Access toolbar. The usual way however is from the **File** 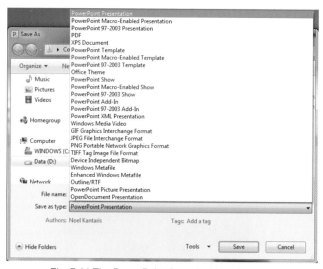 button, which gives you more control of the saving operation.

Clicking the **Save As** option on the Backstage screen, opens the Save As dialogue box from which you can navigate to where you want to save your work. Clicking the down arrow against the **Save as type** box opens a menu of options as shown in Fig. 7.14.

Fig. 7.14 The PowerPoint Save As Type Options

Select **PowerPoint Presentation** if it will only be used in PowerPoint 2010 or 2007. For a presentation that can be opened in either PowerPoint 2010, or earlier versions of PowerPoint, click the **PowerPoint 97-2003 Presentation** option, but you will not be able to use any of the new features available in PowerPoint 2010 or 2007, so beware!

Adding Transitions and Animation

It is easy to add transitions and animation to your presentation to make it more interesting. For example, select the first slide, then click the **Transitions** tab on the Ribbon, click the **More** down-arrow button pointed to in Fig. 7.15, and select the **Rotate** effect to be applied during the transition between the previous slide and the current slide.

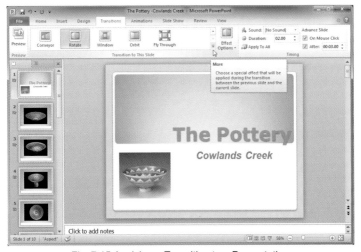

Fig. 7.15 Applying a Transition to a Presentation

Next, click the **Apply to all** button in the **Timing** group, to apply the selected transition to all the slides of the presentation, then set the **Duration** (which is the length of the transition) to 2 seconds, then check the **After** box and set the timing of the **Advance Slide** to 3 seconds, as shown above.

Finally, let us include some animation by clicking the **Animations** tab, selecting the top Placeholder (the one that holds the title), and click the **Add Animation** button on the **Advanced Animation** group, and select the **Fly in** option from the displayed menu shown in Fig. 7.16 on the next page.

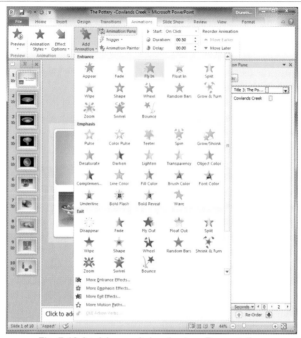

Fig. 7.16 Applying an Animation to a Presentation

Next, set the **Duration** (which is the length of the animation) in the **Timing** group to 0.5 of a second, then click the **Effect Options** button in the **Animation** group and select an appropriate direction from which your animation is to appear.

Finally, repeat the process for the subtitle, and give it a different direction for its appearance. You are now ready to test your efforts by clicking the **Slide Show**, **Start Slide Show**, **From Beginning** command button and enjoy your creation! Do try it using your own pictures. It is the only way to learn!

Fig. 7.17 Selecting an Effect Option

SmartArt Graphics

When you want to illustrate a process, or the relationship between hierarchical elements, you can create a dynamic, visually appealing diagram using SmartArt Graphics. This is a powerful tool available in PowerPoint, Word and Excel. By using predefined sets of formatting, you can easily create the following diagrams:

Process   Visually describe the ordered set of steps required to complete a task.

Hierarchy   Illustrate the structure of an organisation.

Cycle   Represent a circular sequence of steps, tasks or events; or the relationship of a set of steps, tasks or events to a central core element.

Relationship Show convergent, divergent, overlapping or merging elements.

To see some of the many **SmartArt** layouts, click the Placeholder that contains text, then click **SmartArt Tools**, **Design**, **Change Layout**, as shown in Fig. 7.18.

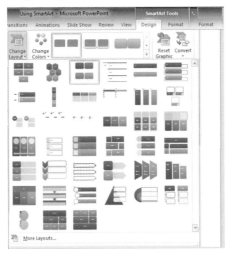

Fig. 7.18 Some of the Many SmartArt Graphics Layouts

Converting Pictures to a SmartArt Graphic

Apart from converting text to a graphic (see next section), PowerPoint 2010 allows you to convert pictures on your presentation slide into a SmartArt graphic, using one of the new, photo-centric SmartArt graphic layouts.

To illustrate the above point, we clicked on the picture of the first slide of our example presentation which displays the **Picture Tools** tab on the Ribbon, then click on **Format**, **Convert to Smart Graphic** button pointed to in Fig. 7.19.

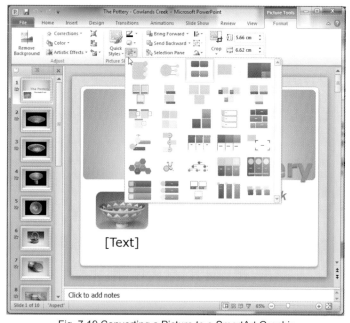

Fig. 7.19 Converting a Picture to a SmartArt Graphic

We selected the third option from the list. As you place the mouse pointer on one of these options, the picture changes to show you how it will look if you choose that option.

Once the SmartArt graphic is created you can move it, re-size it, rotate it, add text to it and change its font and colour. You can also apply animation to it, as you can with all the graphics. This really is an easy process, and the results can be excellent, as shown in Fig. 7.1 on page 141.

Converting Text to a SmartArt Graphic

Let us look at a process of pottery making by inserting bulleted information on a slide (see page 145), before converting it to SmartArt Graphic. First, insert an extra slide at the end of the presentation, then fill in the information given below. Obviously, if you are using a different presentation example, use your own appropriate list.

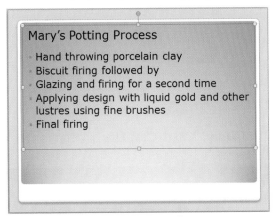

Fig. 7.20 Mary's Potting Process

To convert the above text into a SmartArt graphic, use the **Home**, **Paragraph**, **Convert to SmartArt Graphic** button pointed to in Fig. 7.21 below.

Fig. 7.21 The Convert to SmartArt Graphic Button

Note that for the **Convert to SmartArt Graphic** button to appear in the **Paragraph** group, the Placeholder of the entered text must have been selected by clicking on it, as shown above. Clicking this button displays all the SmartArt Graphics available, as shown in Fig. 7.22 on the next page.

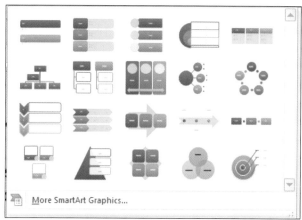

Fig. 7.22 The Available SmartArt Graphics

Clicking the **More Smart Graphics** link opens the screen shown in Fig. 7.23.

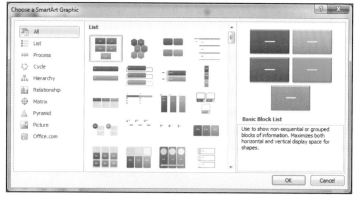

Fig. 7.23 More SmartArt Graphics

The choice is almost endless. As usual, you can see how a SmartArt graphic looks with your text by hovering the mouse pointer over the thumbnail.

We leave it to you to experiment with this type of conversion and to see which SmartArt graphic you prefer. We quite like the **Horizontal Bullet List**, which is the first choice in Fig. 7.22.

PowerPoint Web App

Just as with Word and Excel Web Apps, PowerPoint Web App is part of the Microsoft Web Apps which allows you create presentations on Windows Live. You can then work with such a document directly on the Web site where they are stored.

To use this facility, as we mentioned in the case of Word and Excel, you must set up a Windows Live ID, which is very easy to do and is free! If you already use Hotmail, Messenger or Xbox Live, then you already have a Windows Live ID. If not, use your Internet Explorer and go to the www.live.com Web site, click the **Sign up** link, fill in the required information, then click the **I accept** button.

You can now start using the PowerPoint Web App by saving your latest presentation (**The Pottery**, in our case) to Windows Live SkyDrive. Use the **File**, **Save & Send** command button, then click **Save to Web**, and select **My Documents** (see Fig. 3.26 on page 67). You can also use the **File**, **Save & Send** command to publish a PowerPoint presentation to a Blog site, send it as an attachment to an e-mail, or as a PDF.

To retrieve a PowerPoint presentation from SkyDrive (from anywhere in the World), use your Internet Explorer and go to www.live.com, sign in with your Live ID and Password, click on **Office** and select **Your Documents**, then **My Documents**.

Now, by clicking the required presentation on SkyDrive, it is loaded into PowerPoint Web App, as shown in Fig. 7.24, and then you can use the **File** command button to display a menu of options, such as Open in PowerPoint, Edit in Browser, Share or Start Slide Show.

Fig. 7.24 Loading a Presentation into PowerPoint Web App for Viewing or Printing

Clicking the **Edit in Browser** button in Fig. 7.24, opens the PowerPoint Web App and loads your workbook as shown in Fig. 7.25. As you can see, although the options available on the Ribbon are a limited version to those in PowerPoint, they are quite adequate. We leave it to you to explore.

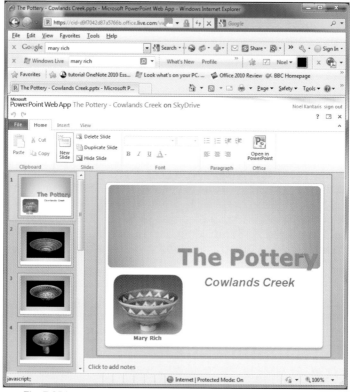

Fig. 7.25 Loading a Document into PowerPoint Web App for Editing

One small criticism: All animation built into a presentation is lost when starting a Slide Show on the Web. The fun is lost!

* * *

PowerPoint 2010 is obviously capable of a lot more than we have introduced here, but you should now be happy to create your own presentations and to explore more of the package by yourself.

8

Microsoft OneNote 2010

OneNote 2010

OneNote is a digital notebook that allows you to gather information in the form of text, Web pages, images, digital handwriting, audio or video recordings.

New and improved features in OneNote 2010 include:

- The adoption of the Ribbon, which keeps consistency across all Office 2010 applications. By default, the Ribbon is minimised when you start OneNote, but displays fully when a Ribbon tab is clicked.

- The facility to share and simultaneously edit Notebooks with colleagues who have permission to do so. OneNote 2010 synchronises all changes made to the shared Notebook in real time, so changes can be seen by all almost immediately.

- The adoption of linked notes, which are placeholders to other items or applications such as Word, Outlook, or a Web page, etc. Linked notes are only supported if you save your Notebook in 2010 format.

- The ability to dock OneNote 2010 to the side of your desktop while you work with other applications. This, together with the ability of linking notes to Web pages makes it easy to find a best deal when shopping online.

- The adoption of a Notebook Recycle Bin to help recover sections or pages of Notebooks that might have been deleted.

- The adoption of right-click context-sensitive menus similar to those in Word, make OneNote easy to use.

Starting the OneNote Program

To start OneNote 2010, use the **Start**, **All Programs** command, select the **Microsoft Office** entry from the displayed menu, and click **Microsoft OneNote 2010**, as shown in Fig. 8.1.

Fig. 8.1 Using the Start Menu

The OneNote Screen

When you start OneNote the program momentarily displays its opening screen, and then displays the last page viewed, or the sample notes, shown here in Fig. 8.2.

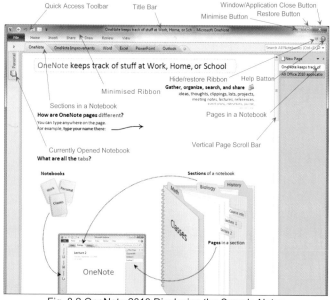

Fig. 8.2 OneNote 2010 Displaying the Sample Notes

On the displayed screen you will see a visual illustration of the various elements that make up OneNote. Whether you have used a previous version of OneNote or not, the first time you use the program, it might be a good idea to refer to this page and the Help System as discussed at the end of Chapter 1. A few minutes might be well spent here. In fact we recommend you study the opening screen, supplied by Microsoft, and watch the video using the link at the end of this OneNote page.

What you see on the screen are three elements that make up OneNote:

- **Notebooks** that display on the left of the screen. In Fig. 8.2 on the previous page, the **Personal** Notebook is shown opened – you can create and display more than one Notebook, but only one can be opened at a time.

- **Sections** that display at the top of the screen as tabs which stretch to accommodate the length of their description. Each Notebook can have several Sections, but your screen might only show one section when you open OneNote for the first time.

- **Pages** and **Sub-pages** that display on the right of the screen. Each section can have as many pages and sub-pages as required.

The Ribbon

When you first start OneNote, the Ribbon is minimised by default, as shown in Fig. 8.2 on the previous page. This gives you more space for your note-taking, but as soon as you click one of its tabs it displays in the normal way. Below we show the Ribbon for the **Home** tab.

Fig. 8.3 The Home Tab of the OneNote 2010 Ribbon

As usual, the Home tab contains all the things you use most often, such as the cut and paste commands, basic text formatting, using styles, tags, etc.

Clicking a new tab opens a new series of groups, each with its relevant command buttons. The content of the other tabs allow you to do the following:

- The Insert tab, displays groupings to enable you to immediately insert Space, Tables, Images, Links, Files, Recordings, Time Stamps and Symbols.

- The Share tab, groups controls for sending Pages, Sections or whole Notebooks by E-mail, Mark changes made to Pages in Notebooks by colleagues as Read, Share Notebooks with friends and colleagues, and keep track of what happened to a Notebook.

- The Draw tab allows the selection of various tools, including drawing pens, the ability of inserting shapes and change their colour.

- The Review tab groups controls for checking the Spelling of your documents and to open the research pane to search through reference materials, translate a page or select a different language and take linked notes in a docked window .

- The View tab allows you to change what you see on the screen. You can choose between Normal View, Full Page View, or Docked to Desktop View, Show or Hide Authors, select different Page Setups, Zoom to different magnifications and control document Windows.

Do note that when you dock OneNote to the desktop (which can also be done from the **Quick Access Toolbar** – see next section), you can only see the page you are using to take notes. Notebooks, Sections, or other Pages are not displayed. This type of display persists even when you change to Full Page View (also achievable from the **Quick Access Toolbar**). To return to the view shown in Fig. 8.2, you must use the **View**, **Normal View** Ribbon command.

To make the Ribbon visible all the time, click the **Expand the Ribbon** ⌄ button, situated to the left of the Help ⑦ button. To minimise the Ribbon, click the **Minimize the Ribbon** ⌃ button.

That is all the content of the fixed Tabs, but there are still others, as described at the bottom of page 5. Some Tabs only appear when they are actually needed. These contextual tabs contain tools that are only active when an object like a picture, chart or equation is selected in the document. These will be covered later as and when they crop up.

Quick Access Toolbar

The Quick Access Toolbar is the small area to the upper left of the Ribbon, as shown in Fig. 8.2, and enlarged here. This is one of the most useful features of

Office 2010. It contains buttons for the things that you use over and over every day, such as **Back**, **Undo**, and **Dock to Desktop**, and **Full Page View**. The bar is always available, whatever you are doing in a program, and it is very easy to add buttons for your most used commands.

Clicking the **Customize Quick Access Toolbar** button pointed to above shows a menu of suggested items for the toolbar. You can select the **More Commands** option In Fig. 8.4, to add others, or even easier, just right-click on a Ribbon control and select **Add to Quick Access Toolbar**.

At this stage, it might be a good idea if you used the **More Commands** option, then on the displayed dialogue box, under **Choose commands from**, select **All commands** and add the **Redo** and **Normal View** commands to the **Quick Access Toolbar**.

Fig. 8.4 Quick Access Options

Context Sensitive Menus

Almost everything you can do with the Ribbon, you can do with context sensitive menus, otherwise known as right-click, or short-cut menus. For example, right-clicking the opened Personal Notebook, displays Fig. 8.5.

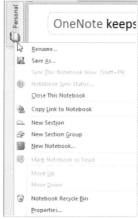

Fig. 8.5 A Notebook Context Sensitive Menu

You can use this particular context sensitive menu to Rename your Notebook, change its contents and Save it by a different name, or create a new Notebook, to mention but a few of the available options.

Similarly, right-clicking a Section tab, displays Fig. 8.6.

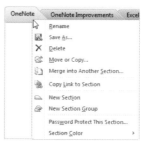

Fig. 8.6 A Section Context Sensitive Menu

In fact, no matter what you are doing in OneNote, there is a context sensitive menu to help you with your task, even when you are entering text. For example, right-clicking on text, displays both a context sensitive menu and the text mini bar, as shown in Fig. 8.7.

All the usual commands associated with text manipulation are available here in the right-click menu, while all the text enhancements you would wish for, are on the mini bar. In fact, we tend to use right-click menus whenever possible!

Fig. 8.7 A Text Context Sensitive Menu and Mini Bar

The OneNote Backstage View

Common with all the other Office 2010 applications, OneNote also uses the  command button to display the Office Backstage view where you can access all the options relating to OneNote and the current document. For example, you can get information on the current document, open an existing document, create a new document, save and print documents.

Creating a New Notebook

To create a new Notebook, click the [File] command button to open the Backstage view, then click the **New** button to display the screen shown in Fig. 8.8.

Fig. 8.8 Creating a New Notebook in OneNote

Note that you must select where you want your new Notebook to be created; on the Web (on SkyDrive), on a Network, or on your Computer. We chose the last option, then gave it a name and location, and clicked the **Create Notebook** button pointed to in Fig. 8.8.

The project we are undertaking here is to find new places, using the Internet, to take our summer visitors near where we live in South West Cornwall. You can create a similar Notebook near where you live. So let us start.

We used Google and typed 'Places to visit in Cornwall UK'. Each section of our Notebook will include different places, such as beaches, heritage sites, gardens, galleries, family attractions and museums. This might be rather ambitious, as we have already found on one Web site alone, 155 beaches, 23 heritage sites, 23 gardens, 38 galleries, 45 family attractions and 21 museums, most of them near us! So, we will limit our example to only two sections and include a couple of pages per section. It is an example, after all!

When you create a new Notebook, what displays in OneNote is shown in Fig. 8.9 below, with the name of the new Notebook on the left (shown open), and one section named **New Section 1**. To give the latter a meaningful name, double-click it to highlight it (or right-click it and select **Rename** from the shortcut menu), and type a new name. We chose to call this section 'Family Attractions'. Also note that this first section has one 'Untitled page' associated with it, which can also be renamed by typing a new name in the oval section above the date.

Fig. 8.9 Renaming a Section and a Page

When you find something on a Web site that interests you, select it by highlighting the portion you want, right-click it, and select the **Send to OneNote** option from the displayed shortcut menu, as shown in Fig. 8.10.

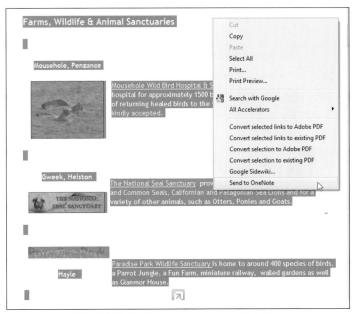

Fig. 8.10 Selecting Information on a Web Site

If you do not select what you want prior to sending information to OneNote, the whole page of that Web site will be transferred over, which perhaps is not your intention.

What appears now in OneNote is shown in Fig. 8.11 on the next page. Note that at the bottom of the OneNote page, a link to the original site from which you obtained the information is included so that you can go back to the Web page at a later stage.

Also note that what we typed in the oval box above the date in Fig. 8.11, appears as a new page name. We used the 'Untitled page' to include a map of the area, thanks to Google Maps, by copying it to the clipboard and pasting it to the Notebook page, then renaming it 'Map of the Area'.

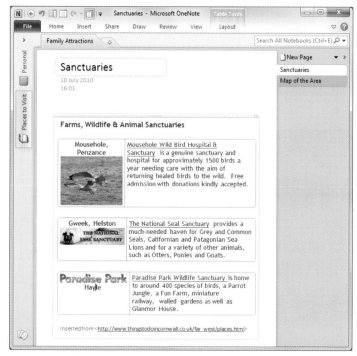

Fig. 8.11 Transferred Information into OneNote

You can change the order in which pages appear in OneNote by dragging a page up or down to a desired position, as shown here in Fig. 8.12.

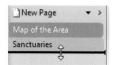

Fig. 8.12 Moving a Page Up or Down

You can also move sections in the same way. Here we illustrate the process by first creating a new section by clicking the **Create a New Section** button, then dragging a selected section right or left to the required position which is marked by a small arrowhead, as shown in Fig. 8.14.

Fig. 8.13 Creating a New Section

Fig. 8.14 Moving a Section Left or Right

Finally, you can demote a page to a sub-page, or promote a sub-page to a page by dragging a page to the right, or a sub-page to the left, as shown in Fig. 8.15.

Fig. 8.15 Demoting or Promoting a Page

Saving a Notebook

To save parts of a Notebook, or the whole Notebook by a different name from the one given to it when first created, or in a different file format (more about this shortly) click the File command button to open the Backstage view, then click the **Save As** button to display the screen shown in Fig. 8.16 below.

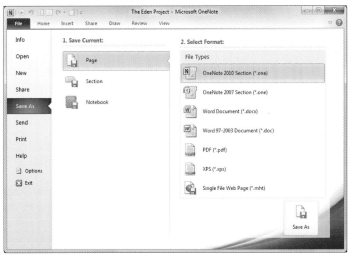

Fig. 8.16 Saving Pages or Sections by a Different File Format

As you can see, it is possible to save sections and pages by making a selection under **Save Current**, then choose one of several different file formats displayed under **Select Format** shown in Fig. 8.16 above. However, when you select to save a whole notebook, the choices under **Select Format** are reduced to **OneNote Package**, **PDF**, or **XPS**.

File Formats in OneNote 2010

OneNote 2010 uses a new type of file format with the extension **.one**. However, saving a OneNote notebook in the 2010 format has the following advantages and implications:

- The new 2010 file format is required for many of the new OneNote features, such as linked note taking, use of mathematical equations, multilevel sub-pages, versioning, Web sharing and using the Recycle Bin to recover deleted notebooks, sections and or pages.

- OneNote 2010 can read and edit OneNote 2007 format notebooks which are opened in 'Compatibility Mode'. When you save such notebooks, they will be saved in OneNote 2007 format so that you can continue to collaborate with colleagues who have not upgraded to OneNote 2010.

- OneNote 2010 file format cannot be used by OneNote 2007 users.

To convert OneNote 2007 file format to OneNote 2010, do the following:

- Right-click the notebook you want to convert and choose **Properties** from the shortcut menu.

- On the displayed Notebook Properties dialogue box, click the **Convert to 2010** button.

To convert OneNote 2010 notebooks to OneNote 2007, use the **Properties** shortcut option, but now click the **Convert to 2007** button in the Notebook Properties dialogue box.

Although OneNote 2010 can open and edit notebooks saved in 2010 or 2007 file format, it can only read notebooks created in OneNote 2003 format. To convert OneNote 2003 to OneNote 2010 or 2007 format, open the notebook in OneNote 2010 and click the Information Bar that appears at the top of every page in the OneNote 2003 notebook. OneNote 2003 notebooks which have been converted to 2010 or 2007 file format cannot be converted back to their original 2003 format.

Using Templates in OneNote

OneNote 2010 allows you to apply built-in templates to the design of new pages, or apply your own custom templates. You also have the option to select from Office.com a variety of templates for notebook, section or page design.

To find and apply a template to a new page in OneNote 2010, do the following:

- Open the notebook or section where you want to add a page and in the page tabs list, click the arrow next to the **New Page** button pointed to here.

- On the drop-down menu, you could either select one of the displayed page designs, or click the **Page Templates** option to open the Template task pane.

- In the Templates task pane, to use one of the built-in page templates, expand the type of template that you prefer, and then click the template of your choice, as shown in Fig. 8.17.

- To find a template on Office.com, click the **Templates on Office.com** option, then click a template category, select the template that you want, and click **Download** to download it to your computer.

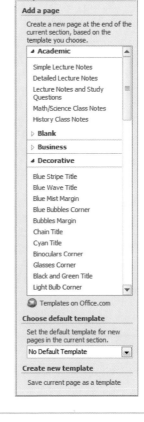

Fig. 8.17 Selecting a Page Template

Searching Notebooks

One of the biggest advantages of an electronic notebook over a paper one, is the ability to search for information quickly and easily. Not only can you search one specified notebook, but you can also choose to search all your notebooks, or restrict your search to sections, or pages.

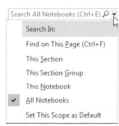

Fig. 8.18 Where to Search

By default OneNote searches all notebooks, as shown here in the Search box, but it can be changed by clicking the down-arrow pointed to in Fig. 8.18, which opens a menu of options.

To start a search, type what you want to search for, say 'New' and click the **Search** 🔍 button. You will notice that as you type each letter in the **Search** box, results appear on a screen to the right of it. At the very bottom of that screen, click the option **Open Search Results Page**. What now displays on screen is shown in Fig. 8.19.

As you can see, every occurrence of the word 'New' in all of our notebooks is displayed here. This is a very powerful facility and is worth exploring further. We leave it to you!

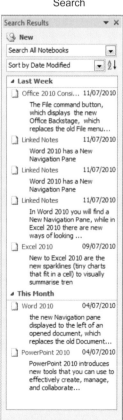

Fig. 8.19 Search Results

Getting Help with OneNote

Whether you have used a previous version of OneNote or not, there is a lot of help to make it easy for you to either migrate from a previous version, or get to grips with the application for the first time.

To start the Help system, click the **Help** button on the Ribbon, or press the **F1** keyboard key. These open the Get Help Using Microsoft Office window, provided you are connected to the Internet, as shown in Fig. 8.20.

It is worth looking at the **Get Started with OneNote 2010** first, then click the **OneNote Demos** entry to display a feast of demos, most of which are shown in Fig. 8.21.

Fig. 8.20 The Microsoft Office Help Window

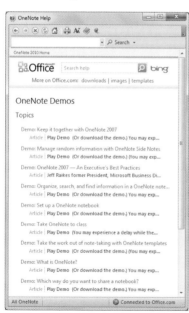

Fig. 8.21 The Microsoft OneNote Demo List

Some of these were from OneNote 2007, but are still worth exploring. If you are not connected to the Internet, you'll only get the OneNote Help window which is also worth exploring.

Taking Linked Notes

Sometimes it is useful to make notes while you are working with other Office 2010 applications or the Internet Explorer. OneNote 2010 allows you to do that by letting you take notes in a docked OneNote window. While you take notes in this way, OneNote stores with each paragraph, picture, or Web page, a link to the original document or site so that you can return to it later. However, to use the linked note facility your notebook must be saved in the OneNote 2010 file format.

As an illustration we will take linked notes on a Word document, the opening page of the PowerPoint presentation we created in Chapter 7, a picture of the view from Cowlands Pottery found on the Web, and a new section in the notebook we created in OneNote, as shown in Fig. 8.22.

To create linked notes do the following:

- Dock OneNote to the desktop.

- Start Word, PowerPoint, or OneNote, then on the Ribbon in the **Review** tab, click the **Link Notes** button.

- In the **Select Location in OneNote** dialogue box, navigate to the notebook you want to use.

- As you type notes in OneNote, a small graphic appears on the left margin of what you are typing indicating the application you are using.

- To link notes to a Web page, click the **Tools** button and select the **OneNote Linked Notes** from the displayed drop-down menu.

Here, we highlighted all the entries of the linked notes so you can see all the small graphics of the applications used when entering these notes. Clicking a graphic opens the original document in its application.

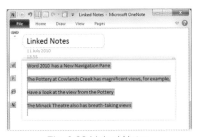

Fig. 8.22 Linked Notes

OneNote Web App

Just as with Word, Excel, and PowerPoint Web Apps, OneNote uses this facility to create and maintain notebooks on Windows Live. You can then edit such notebooks directly on the Web site where they are stored.

To use this facility, as we mentioned in the case of Word, Excel, and PowerPoint, you must set up a Windows Live ID, which is very easy to do and is free! If you already use Hotmail, Messenger, or Xbox Live, then you already have a Windows Live ID. If not, use your Internet Explorer and go to the www.live.com Web site, click the **Sign up** link, fill in the required information, then click the **I accept** button.

You can now start using the OneNote Web App by saving your latest notebook (**Places to Visit**, in our case) to Windows Live SkyDrive. Use the **File**, **Share** command button, then under **Share on** select **Web**, then under **Web Location** select **My Documents**, as shown in Fig. 8.23.

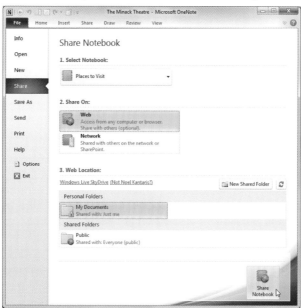

Fig. 8.23 Sending a Notebook to SkyDrive

When you first select the notebook you want to send to the SkyDrive, you are asked to specify the drive and folder where it is to be 'Unpacked'. We used the **Office 2010 Docs** folder on the D: drive. After the unpacking process, it is sent to the Skydrive and is synchronised with original notebook.

To retrieve a notebook from SkyDrive, use the Internet Explorer and go to www.live.com, sign in with your Live ID and Password, click on **Office** and select **Your Documents**, then **My Documents**, and click the notebook you want to load into OneNote Web App. In Fig. 8.24, we show our 'Places to Visit' notebook opened in the OneNote Web App.

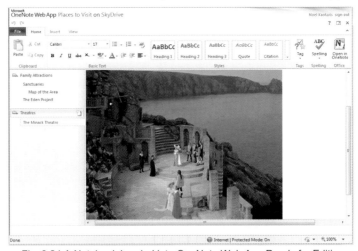

Fig. 8.24 A Notebook Loaded into OneNote Web App Ready for Editing

As you can see, although the Ribbon on the OneNote Web App is not as extensive as that of the OneNote 2010 application, it is sufficient for most purposes. Unfortunately, when we uploaded the notebook 'Linked Notes', the actual links to the application of their origin, were not there!

* * *

OneNote 2010 is obviously capable of a lot more than we have discussed here, but you should now be happy and able to create your own notebooks and to explore more of the package by yourself.

9

Microsoft Outlook 2010

Microsoft's Outlook 2010 is a powerful electronic communication and personal information manager – like an e-mail program with a Filofax built in. To use it effectively your computer needs to be connected to the Internet or to a shared network resource, the latter being essential if you are planning to use Outlook's group-scheduling features.

Starting Outlook 2010

Fig. 9.1 The Microsoft Office List of Applications

Outlook 2010 is started in Windows by using the **Start**, **All Programs** command, selecting the **Microsoft Office** entry from the displayed menu and clicking on **Microsoft Outlook 2010**, shown in Fig. 9.1.

In Windows 7 we prefer to place the **Outlook** icon on the Taskbar by right-clicking the Outlook entry (Fig. 9.1) and selecting the **Pin to Taskbar** option from the displayed list. This allows for a one-click access to Outlook, as shown in Fig. 9.2.

Fig. 9.2 The Microsoft Outlook Icon on the Taskbar

Fig. 9.3 The Microsoft Outlook 2010 Starting Box

When you start Outlook 2010 the program momentarily displays a Starting box, shown in Fig. 9.3, and opens with a display that may look something like that shown in Fig. 9.4 below. By default, the Ribbon is minimised when you first start the program, but displays when a tab is clicked.

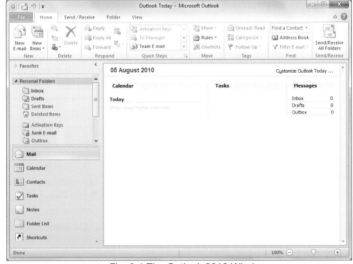

Fig. 9.4 The Outlook 2010 Window

The first thing you will notice is that the Office 2010 graphic interface, the Ribbon, has been implemented in Outlook 2010 as well. We shall be discussing this shortly.

What you see may not be the same as we show above, depending on the settings you have active. Below the Ribbon the window is split into two areas at present – which will change the moment you click one of the **Personal Folders** in the **Mail** activity, or one of the other activities, such as Calendar, Contacts, etc. The windows of the various activities of Outlook will be different, but for the time being we will concentrate on **Mail**.

Parts of the Outlook Screen

At the top of the **Mail** screen (Figs 9.4 & 9.5) is the Ribbon, while to the left of the screen is the Navigation Pane, the upper part of which controls what is displayed in the centre working area of the Outlook window.

On the lower part of the Navigation pane you will find buttons that open activities such as **Mail**, **Calendar**, **Contacts**, **Tasks** and **Notes**, as well as **Folder List** and **Shortcuts** options. Clicking any of these Outlook activity buttons displays related screens.

With the **Mail** activity selected, clicking the **Inbox** folder displays the screen below.

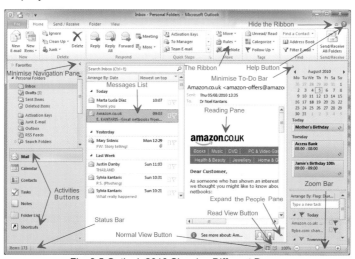

Fig. 9.5 Outlook 2010 Showing Different Panes

If you press the **Alt** key on the keyboard, a set of shortcut keys are displayed on the Ribbon. Try it to see for yourself. The Reading area at the centre of the screen is where you read your e-mail messages, but at present is rather small. To substantially increase it, click the **Minimise Navigation Pane** and **To-Do Bar** buttons, and make sure that the **People** pane is collapsed. What now displays is shown in Fig. 9.6 on the next page.

Fig. 9.6 The Enlarged Reading Pane Area

Note that the **Minimise** buttons have now been replaced by **Maximise** buttons. Clicking the **Normal** button at the bottom of Fig. 9.5, returns the Outlook window to its former state, as shown in Fig. 9.5, while clicking the **Reading** button (to the right of the **Normal** button) is a quick way of collapsing the **Navigation** and the **To-Do** panes, as well as the Ribbon area.

The Ribbon

Traditional menus and toolbars have been replaced in Outlook 2010 by the Ribbon – a new device in this version of Outlook that presents commands organised into a set of tabs, as discussed in Chapter 1 and shown in Fig.9.7 below.

Fig. 9.7 The Home Tab of the Outlook 2010 Ribbon

The tabs on the Ribbon display the commands that are most relevant for each of the task areas in an Outlook Activity, as shown above for **Mail**.

The Navigation Pane

In Outlook 2010 the Navigation Pane appears in all views by default. It forms an easy way of letting you navigate to different Outlook features by clicking buttons, shortcuts or folders. You can re-size or hide it, or display it in a minimised form to use less screen space.

The contents of the Navigation Pane change depending on what view (such as Mail or Calendar) you are using. Each view offers access to Outlook information relevant to that view.

The view buttons at the lower part of the Navigation Pane correspond to Outlook's different views, or activity areas, such as Calendar, Tasks or Contacts. Depending on the view that you choose, you see a different set of panes, folders, and information. Furthermore, you can add or remove buttons as and when they are needed.

Fig. 9.8 Different Navigation Pane Configurations

To re-size the Navigation Pane point to the right border and when the pointer becomes a double-headed arrow ⬌, drag it to the left or right.

The buttons in the Navigation Pane open the following Outlook 2010 views when they are clicked:

Mail   The Mail activity where you read and send e-mail messages and feeds.

Calendar   The Calendar and Scheduling activity in which you can create and manage appointments, meetings and events.

Contacts   The activity that accesses an address book of contact details.

Tasks   Used to manage tasks and small projects.

Notes   Used to make and manage 'stick on' type notes.

Folder List Displays your mail folders in the Navigation Pane when you switch to other activities.

Shortcuts   Gives quick access to your favourite folders or to Web pages.

Journal   Keeps a record of any interaction that you want to remember, such as tracking e-mail messages or meetings.

The View Tab

You can configure the display of the various Outlook activities by using the View tab on the Ribbon. This opens the screen shown in Fig. 9.9 on the next page.

It is worth spending some time here trying the various display views to see which suits you best. As you can see there are several options to choose from.

The To-Do Bar

The To-Do Bar is worth its weight in gold. You can keep it open in all Outlook 2010 activities, so you can see and work with your Tasks list, e-mail messages you have flagged for follow-up and your appointments, even when you are working in the Tasks, Mail or one of the other Outlook activities.

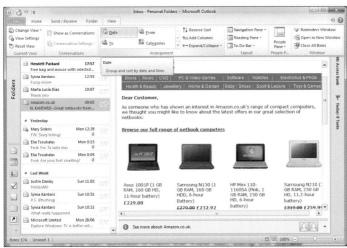

Fig. 9.9 Using the View Tab to Configure your Display

By default, the To-Do bar is closed in the Calendar activity, but you can activate it from the View tab, using the **To-Do** command in the **Layout** group of the Ribbon and selecting **Normal** from the list of options. Once opened in this way the To-Do bar will stay open whenever you use Calendar until

you either minimise it or close it by selecting **Off** in the options list of the **To-Do** command in the **Layout** group on the View tab of the Ribbon.

The To-Do bar consists of four parts, as shown in Fig. 9.10. These are:

- The Date Navigator, which shows a small calendar display which you can click to set the active date.

Fig. 9.10 Parts of the To-Do Bar

- The Appointments section, which shows what you have planned for the next few days.

- The Task Input Panel where you can quickly add your tasks that need doing.

- The Task list at the bottom of the bar, where your tasks, messages and contacts that have been flagged are shown.

You can turn each part on or off by right-clicking the To-Do bar, and then clicking the part you want to turn on or off.

Importing Data into Outlook

In our experience when Office 2010 is installed it does a good job of finding and including your previous e-mail settings, data and saved messages, especially if you previously used an older version of Outlook or Outlook Express.

If you also hold personal or business information, such as contacts or tasks to perform, on another program, it is easy to import these into Outlook as well, by using the **File** button on the Ribbon and selecting the **Open** command and clicking the **Import** option as shown in Fig. 9.11.

Fig. 9.11 Selecting the Import Option from the Backstage View

This starts the Import and Export Wizard, the first screen of which is shown in Fig. 9.12.

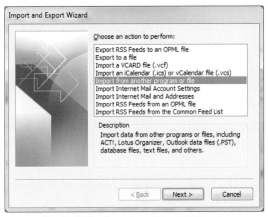

Fig. 9.12 The Import and Export Wizard

Next, highlight the **Import from another program or file** entry and press **Next**, which displays a list of possible organiser-type formats that it can handle as shown in Fig. 9.13.

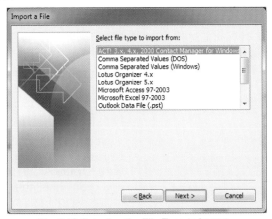

Fig. 9.13 Selecting the File Type to Import

If the file type to import appears on the list above, all is well. Just select it and tell the Wizard on the next screen where to find it.

However, if the file type does not appear in the list, then you will have to go back to your previously used organiser and export the data into **Comma Separated Values**, so that you can use this file type to import your data into Outlook.

Having selected the type of file you want to convert, pressing the **Next** button displays the next Wizard screen in which you are asked to locate the file to be converted. After that the conversion is automatic – just follow the on-screen instructions.

We found the data conversion to be faultless. We were particularly impressed that the extensive information in our **Contacts** folder was converted fully and accurately. Obviously we cannot show you the outcome of this process, as it contains private and sensitive information, but you may see some conversion entries as we examine the individual sections of Outlook in later pages.

Getting Help

To find out more about Outlook in general, and its new features in particular, press the **F1** key or left-click the **Microsoft Outlook Help** button on the extreme right of the Ribbon, and shown here. This opens the Help window shown in Fig. 9.14.

The font size of the help items can be changed by clicking the ⒶⓍ icon pointed to in Fig. 9.14.

Now you can either choose the **Getting started with Outlook 2010** link, or you can use the **Search** facility to look up something else (if it exists). Try typing 'instant help' into the text box and clicking **Search**.

Fig. 9.14 The Outlook Help Screen

This opens the Help window displaying the Search results found for your question, which in this case should include the entry 'What's new in Microsoft Outlook 2010'. We suggest you look up this topic, even if you are an experienced Outlook user. Perhaps you might learn something new!

E-mail with Microsoft Outlook

| Mail | It is most likely that you will spend most of your time with Outlook 2010 dealing with e-mail messages. For this to work we have assumed that your computer is connected to the Internet, or a local area network (LAN), so that you can receive e-mail. A connection to the Internet is usually made via a modem and a telephone line, an ethernet card to a LAN which itself is connected to the Internet, an ISDN direct line, or Broadband connection. The last two provide faster connections, and since they now are cheaper have become the most popular.

To use a telephone based connection you will need to subscribe to an Internet Service Provider (ISP) which is a company that allows you to connect to its Internet host. There are many of these in the UK. Most can be found in adverts in one of the many computer magazines. Be careful though before committing yourself to one provider as the quality of service and costs can vary considerably. One thing we can't do here is make specific recommendations, but try and find the opinion of someone who uses the company you decide on, or have a trial period with them.

All ISPs offer an e-mail address and a mailbox facility to hold your incoming messages until you connect and download them to your computer so that you can read them. As long as your computer can access the Internet, you can use e-mail to keep in touch with friends and colleagues, anywhere in the world, provided they have their own e-mail address. The whole procedure of connecting to your ISP, downloading e-mail, filtering unwanted junk e-mail, saving and managing e-mail and other information, such as addresses of Web sites, can be done very easily in Outlook 2010 – we will step you through the procedures later.

Using Folders

Fig. 9.15 Outlook Mail Folders

Most of the default Mail folders in Outlook 2010 are self-explanatory and are shown here in Fig. 9.15. They are placed in the Personal Folders section by Outlook.

Inbox is the folder containing all your received e-mails (4 unread messages in this case), **Draft** contains any messages under preparation that you intend to complete later, and **Outbox** is the folder containing prepared e-mail messages which are waiting to be sent.

Other folders are used for housekeeping, such as the **Deleted Items** folder used to hold deleted items before you finally clear them from your system or reinstate them. The **Sent Items** folder holds a copy of all e-mail messages you have sent. The **Junk E-mail** folder can be made to hold filtered junk e-mail, and **Search Folders** hold specified e-mail searches, so that you can use them again. **RSS Feeds** contains any live Feeds that you have subscribed to. **RSS** stands for 'Real Simple Syndication'. Here, we have also created a folder called **Activation Keys** to hold all the e-mail messages we have been sent by software suppliers containing information relating to activation keys for the purchased software. You may have something similar.

As you receive new e-mail messages, unless they are filtered out they are all placed in the **Inbox**. Perhaps most of them you will delete, but you will want to save some for future reference. This means the **Inbox** gets bigger and bigger. You might like to create folders to hold your stored messages, in some sort of order, like our **Activation Keys** folder. You might, for example create folders to hold e-mail messages from specific members of your family, or messages dealing with a specific business, etc.

Creating a New Folder

You can add new folders, under a selected folder, by clicking the Folder tab on the Ribbon, then clicking the **New Folder** command, pointed to in Fig. 9.16, which opens the box shown in Fig. 9.17 for you to fill in the details.

Fig. 9.16 Creating a New Mail Folder

Fig. 9.17 The Create New Folder Dialogue Box

You enter the new folder **Name** and what the **Folder contains**. Here, as can be seen in Fig. 9.17, the **Inbox** folder is selected, therefore on pressing the **OK** button the new folder will become a sub-folder of that folder.

Had we selected the Personal Folders item instead of the **Inbox** folder, prior to clicking the **New Folder** command, the new folder would have appeared in the main listing, like the **Activation Keys** folder, also shown in Fig. 9.17.

You can move and copy messages from one folder into another. To move a message, you just select its header line in the Messages List and with the left mouse button depressed 'drag' it to the folder in the Folders List. When you release the mouse button, the message will be moved to that folder.

The copy procedure is very much the same, except you must also have the **Ctrl** key depressed when you release the mouse button. You can tell which operation is taking place by looking at the mouse pointer. It will show a '+' when copying, as on the right.

Dragging folders is fast but it is easy to accidentally 'drop' messages in the wrong location. It may be safer to right-click messages you want to move, and select **Move to Folder** from the displayed context menu. You then select the folder name from the list of folders in the Move Items dialogue box and click **OK**. Which method you use is up to you, but we usually use 'drag and drop' ourselves.

E-mail Accounts

Outlook supports several types of e-mail accounts.

Microsoft Exchange – An e-mail based communications server often used by networked businesses. Home users typically do not have an Exchange account so cannot use the features in Outlook that require Exchange.

POP3 – A common protocol that is used to retrieve e-mail messages from an Internet e-mail server.

IMAP – **I**nternet **M**essage **A**ccess **P**rotocol – Creates folders on a server to store and organise messages for retrieval by other computers. You can read message headers only and select which messages to download.

HTTP – Web-based e-mail service, such as Windows Live Mail.

If you are lucky, Outlook will have recognised and set up your e-mail account when the program was installed. That was certainly the case with us. For most accounts, Outlook 2010 can automatically detect and configure the account by using just a name, an e-mail address, and a password. Exchange account users usually don't have to type any information, because Outlook 2010 identifies the network credentials used to connect to the Exchange account.

If the identification fails, you will have to start the process manually. Your e-mail administrator or Internet service provider (ISP) should have provided you with the configuration information you need to proceed. If not, you will need to get in touch with them.

In Outlook, e-mail accounts are included in profiles, where a profile consists of accounts, data files, and settings containing details about where your e-mail is stored. A new profile is created automatically when you run Outlook for the first time, and after that the profile runs each time that you start Outlook. You can have several e-mail accounts in a single Outlook user profile. You could add an Exchange account to handle your business e-mail and then add a POP3 account from your ISP, for your personal e-mail.

Adding a New Account

To add a new e-mail account to your profile, click the button, then click the **Account Settings** icon highlighted in Fig. 9.18, to display an additional button, as shown below.

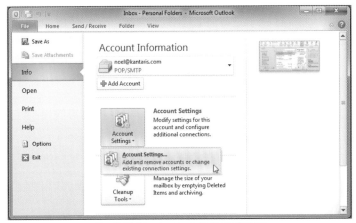

Fig. 9.18 The Account Settings Button

Clicking this second button, pointed to above, opens the dialogue box shown in Fig. 9.19 on the next page, in which you can create, or remove e-mail accounts or change the settings of existing ones.

Next, click **New** to open the dialogue box shown in Fig. 9.20, also displayed on the next page, select the Service you want; **E-mail Account**, **Text Messaging**, or **Other**, and then click the **Next** button.

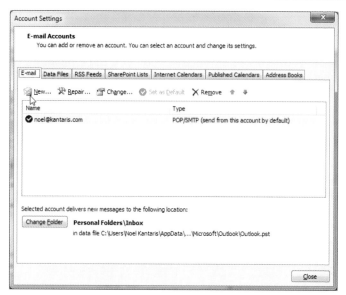

Fig. 9.19 Adding a New E-mail Account

Fig. 9.20 Choosing an E-mail Service

Clicking the **Next** button opens the Auto Account Setup dialogue box, as shown in Fig. 9.21 on the next page.

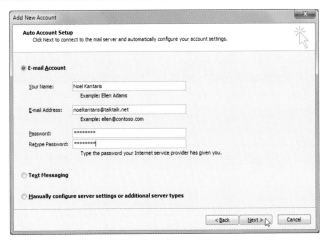

Fig. 9.21 The Auto Account Setup Box

This is where you enter the information for your account. In the **Your Name** box, type your name as you want it to appear to other people. In the **E-mail Address** box, type the complete e-mail address as obtained from your mail administrator or ISP. In the two **Password** boxes, type the password for your mail account followed by the **Next** button. Hopefully the rest is automatic and results in the following.

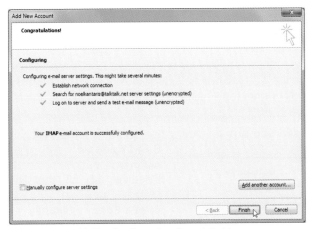

Fig. 9.22 The Configuration Complete Message

Your e-mail server is contacted and Outlook is configured for your account. If an encrypted connection cannot be established to the e-mail server, as in our case, you are prompted to click **Next** to attempt an unencrypted connection. After your account is configured successfully, and you click the **Finish** button you should find a new message in Outlook confirming that all is as it should be.

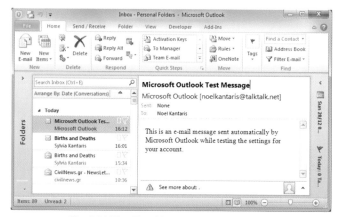

Fig. 9.23 The Test Message Sent by Outlook

This new semi-automatic procedure is a great improvement and makes setting up e-mail accounts very easy indeed. You only need three pieces of information, your name, your e-mail address and password. Outlook does the rest.

If you attempt to include a Windows Live e-mail account in Outlook 2010, you will be advised to download the Windows Outlook connector – a link to the download site is provided.

You are now in a position to send and receive e-mail. Provided you are still connected to the Internet, clicking the

Fig. 9.24 The Send/Receive All Folders Command Button

Send/Receive All Folders command button in the Send / Receive tab of the Ribbon, shown here in Fig. 9.24, downloads instantly any messages you might have waiting for you in your e-mail accounts.

Creating and Sending E-mail Messages

The best way to test out new e-mail features is to send a test message to your own e-mail address. This saves wasting somebody else's time, and the message can be very quickly checked to see the results. So, click the **New E-mail** command button on the Home tab of the Ribbon to open a new Message window shown in Fig. 9.25.

Note the address in the **To...** box is shown underlined. This was automatically done by Outlook after we typed in the text string and moved to the **Subject:** box, because it is recognised as an e-mail address by Outlook. Later on we will discuss how to choose an address from Contacts.

Fig. 9.25 A Test E-mail in Outlook 2010's Message Window

Each e-mail should have a short subject, which is what will appear on the Messages List when the message is received. The **Cc** box is where you include the address of additional persons that you would like to receive a copy of the same message. To send the message, simply press the **Send** button which closes the Message window. If you are connected to the Internet, the message will be sent immediately. If not it will be placed in the **Outbox**, waiting for you to go online.

In a few moments (just over 2 minutes in our case), the message appeared in the **Inbox**, as in Fig. 9.26 on the next page.

You can click the **Send/Receive All Folders** command button on the Send / Receive tab to force Outlook to check the mailbox.

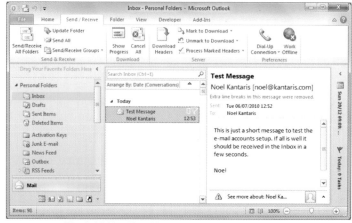

Fig. 9.26 The Test Message Received in our Inbox

As you can see, the contents of a selected message in the Messages List appear in Outlook's Reading Pane. Here the Reading Pane appears to the right of the Messages List. Double-clicking an e-mail title, opens the message in its own Message window.

Outlook's Message Formats

Outlook 2010 supports three types of message formats:

HTML   This message format can produce highly formatted messages with different fonts, colours, bullet lists and graphics.

Plain text A format supported by all e-mail programs, but does not support text formatting or display graphics in the body of the message, but pictures can be included as attachments.

RTF   A Rich Text Format used by Microsoft Office programs like Outlook.

Outlook 2010 automatically converts RTF formatted messages to HTML by default when you send them to an Internet recipient, so that the message formatting is maintained and attachments are received. However, try to avoid excessive text enhancement as there are still some people out there who use e-mail programs that are only capable of receiving plain text, and therefore, not everyone will be able to read the work you spent ages creating!

When you reply to a message in Outlook 2010 it automatically uses the same format as the original message. So if someone sends you a message in Plain Text, your reply will be created in Plain Text.

Formatting Text

There are several ways to format the text of your message. You can use the various command buttons on the **Message** tab, in the **Basic Text** group, and on the **Format Text** tab, in the **Font** group and the **Styles** group.

Also, you can format text using the Mini toolbar or the drop-down list of options that appears when you select text in the message and click the right mouse button. You can change the font, increase or decrease the size by one increment, select a theme, use the Format Painter, select the font style (bold, italic and underline), highlight text, select from a variety of paragraph styles, insert a hyperlink, look up the spelling of the text, find a synonym and translate a word or a phrase from English to another language.

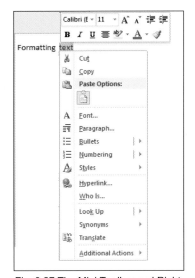

Fig. 9.27 The Mini Toolbar and Right-click Options

Adding Graphics

On the **Insert** tab, in the **Illustrations** group, you can add **Picture**s from a file, **ClipArt**, ready made **Shapes**, to visually communicate information and **Chart**s to illustrate and compare data. In the **Tables** group you can add a **Table**. We leave it to you to experiment with these features.

Including graphics in a message can have startling visual results but can also increase the file size of your e-mail message, so it will take longer to send and to receive.

* * *

In the next chapter, amongst other topics, we shall discuss how to respond to e-mail messages, create e-mail signatures, deal with junk mail, search folders, and how to send graphics as e-mail attachments.

* * *

10

Other E-mail Features

Selecting Options Settings

Now that we have finished experimenting with sending and receiving the first e-mail, it is a good idea to make some permanent changes to Outlook's settings. Use the File button on the Ribbon, and click the **Options** command pointed to in Fig. 10.1 below.

Fig. 10.1 The File Backstage View

This opens the Office Options dialogue box, and selecting **Mail** on the left pane, displays the Outlook Options screen shown in Fig. 10.2 on the next page. We suggest you make the following selections:

- Make sure that the **Always check spelling before sending** option is ticked, so that every message you write is checked before it is sent.

- Click the [Spelling and Autocorrect...] button and check or change the default options for spelling and auto-correcting.

- Scroll down to **Replies and forwards**. In the **When replying to a message** and **When forwarding a message** list boxes you can select to include or not include the original message with your reply.

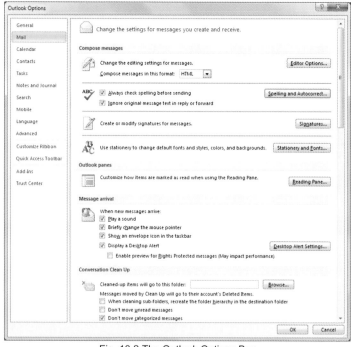

Fig. 10.2 The Outlook Options Box

To implement any changes made in this dialogue box, click the **OK** button. Obviously there are a lot more selections you could make, but we leave these to you. Very soon, after you have been using Outlook 2010 for a while, you will know yourself what options and preferences to choose.

Spell Checking E-mail Messages

Just because e-mail messages are a quick way of getting in touch with friends and family, there is no reason why they should be full of spelling mistakes, as Outlook 2010 is linked to the spell checker that comes with Microsoft Office. Misspelled words that cannot be corrected automatically by Outlook, will be underlined in red, as shown in Fig. 10.3 below.

Do try it out by preparing a message in the New Message window, but with obvious spelling mistakes, as shown below.

Right-clicking a flagged 'error' opens a drop-down menu. You can accept a suggestion, **Ignore All** occurrences, or add your original word to the dictionary for future use. This works very well. However, make sure that the spelling of an added word is correct, otherwise you will end up with a dictionary full of misspelled words!

Fig. 10.3 Correcting Spelling Mistakes

Using the Thesaurus

If you are not sure of the meaning of a word, or you want to use an alternative word in your e-mail, then the thesaurus is an indispensable tool.

Simply place the cursor on the word you want to look up and click the **Review**, **Proofing**, **Thesaurus** button, shown in Fig. 10.4. This opens the Research Task Pane, and as long as the word is recognised, synonyms are listed, as shown below.

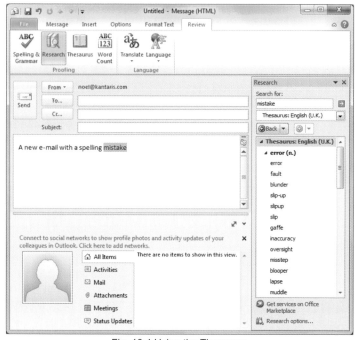

Fig. 10.4 Using the Thesaurus

You can use the thesaurus like a simple dictionary by typing any word into the **Search for** box and clicking the 🔁 button. Again, if the word is recognised, lists of its meaning variations and synonyms will be displayed.

A quick way to get a list of alternatives to a word in your e-mail is to right-click it and select **Synonyms** from the drop-down menu. If you select one from the list it will replace the original word. The last choice in the list activates the **Thesaurus**.

Incoming E-mail Messages

As we saw earlier (see Fig. 9.6 on page 180), you can get a quick overview of an incoming e-mail message by selecting its header in the Messages List and looking at its contents in the Reading Pane. However, it is easier to work with your messages in the Message window, shown in Fig. 10.5. This is opened by double-clicking the message header in the Messages List, or with the **Ctrl+O** keyboard shortcut.

Fig. 10.5 Viewing a Message in its Own Window

As you can see, in this view Outlook uses a cut-down version of the Ribbon. Also, by default, Outlook 2010 deactivates links to pictures in received e-mail messages until you have checked and given your permission to display them. This is because some 'spammers' (people who send masses of unsolicited e-mail messages) use such pictures to prove to themselves that an e-mail address is alive.

Responding to a Message

Fig. 10.6 Responding

Some messages will require some sort of answer or response action, which you carry out from the **Respond** group on the Ribbon.

To reply to the original sender, click **Reply**. To reply to the sender and everyone else who received the message, click **Reply to All**. A new already addressed Message window is opened, for you to type your reply and click **Send**. By default, when you reply to an e-mail message, the original message text is included at the end of the message body.

To forward a message to somebody else, click **Forward** and enter their name in the **To...** box. You can also add recipient names to the **Cc...** and **Bcc...** boxes, to send copies and 'blind copies'. You use **Bcc...** if you don't want anyone else to know that the recipient was sent a copy. Underhand?

Filing Actions

Even if an e-mail message doesn't require a direct response, it may need some sort of filing action, such as deleting unwanted messages from the **Delete** Ribbon group, shown in Fig. 10.7, and saving or printing which is carried out from the **File** button menu shown in Fig. 10.8 below.

Fig. 10.7

Fig. 10.8
Outlook's File
Menu

Deleted items are held in the **Deleted Items** folder, in case you want to resurrect them. To empty this folder, right-click it in the Folders List and select the **Empty Folder** option from the drop-down menu pointed to in Fig. 10.9

Fig. 10.9 The Empty Folder Option

Flagging Messages

When a message will need some sort of future action, either

Unread/ Categorize Follow
Read   Up

Tags

Fig. 10.10 The
Tags Group

right-click the greyed flag against its header on the Message List, or click the **Follow Up** button (Fig. 10.10) which displays when you click the **Home**, **Tags** button. Both actions display the drop-down menu shown in Fig. 10.11 which allows you to attach a 'flag' to the message header.

Today

Tomorrow

This Week

Next Week

No Date

Custom...

Add Reminder...

✓ Mark Complete

Clear Flag

Set Quick Click...

Fig. 10.11
Date Options

Messages that you flag for follow-up also show in the To-Do Bar, in the Task List, and on your Calendar. Also, you can set reminders for them so that you actually remember to do the follow-up.

Categories

You might also want to attach coloured categories to your messages. This makes them more visible and easier to sort.

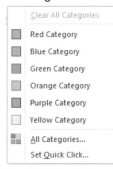

Clear All Categories

Red Category

Blue Category

Green Category

Orange Category

Purple Category

Yellow Category

All Categories...

Set Quick Click...

Fig. 10.12 The Coloured
Categories Menu

At first, Outlook categories do not have proper names, only Red Category, Orange Category, etc., as shown in Fig. 10.12. When you first use one of these, Outlook prompts you to rename it. You could create names such as Holiday, Birthdays, etc.

To give a category to a message you click the **Categorize** button, shown above in Fig. 10.10.

Another way to assign a colour category to a message is to right-click the Categories column (greyed oblong) on the Messages List and use the displayed shortcut menu.

Once you have assigned a category to a message, you can quickly scan your **Inbox** and find the message just by looking for its coloured tag.

Other Follow Up Actions

We saw in a previous section that you can drag a message from the Messages List to the To-Do Bar to create a Task. You can also drag messages from the Messages List to the appropriate button on the Navigation Pane. What the result is depends on which button you use.

To set up a meeting, drag the message to the Calendar button on the Navigation Pane. A new appointment opens for you to fill in the rest of the details, such as the date, time and location of the meeting. All you need to do then is invite the person to the meeting, and click **Send**.

When you drag a message to the **Contacts** button on the Navigation Pane, a new Contact form opens and the e-mail address in the message is automatically added to it. If you like, you can then fill in the rest of the details, such as an address and phone numbers.

With both these actions, dragging creates a new item, but leaves the message still in your **Inbox**. You need to delete it yourself if you don't need it any more.

Moving Between Messages

When you are working with individual e-mail messages in their own Message window you can easily move to the previous or next message in the list. The Quick Access toolbar has two buttons for this, as shown in Fig. 10.13.

Fig. 10.13 The Quick Access Toolbar

Clicking the **Previous Item** button, as shown above, will open messages moving up the listing. Clicking the **Next Item** button opens the next message in the messages list.

You might find it useful to remember the keyboard shortcuts for these actions:

Previous Item	**Ctrl+<**
Next Item	**Ctrl+>**

Desktop Alerts

By default Outlook flashes a desktop message briefly whenever:

* A new message is placed in the **Inbox** as shown in Fig. 10.14. The alert displays the name of the sender, the subject and the first two lines of the message.

* A meeting request is received. The alert displays the sender, subject, date, time and location of the meeting.

* A task request is received. The alert displays the sender, subject and start date of the assigned task.

Fig. 10.14 Desktop Alert of an Incoming E-mail

Desktop Alerts appear whatever you are doing on your PC, but provided Outlook is minimised on the Task bar. As long as you move quickly, you can perform several actions without opening the message. You can move it, set a flag, delete the message, mark it as read, or open a Settings box and customise how the Alert operates, as shown below in the composite of Fig. 10.15.

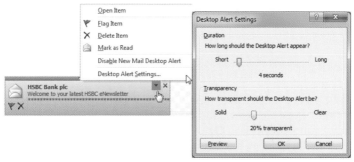

Fig. 10.15 Controlling the Performance of Desktop Alerts

If you need to keep a Desktop Alert visible so that you can read it, place the pointer on it before it fades away.

To turn off alerts, select the **Disable New Desktop Alert** button on the drop-down menu (Fig. 10.15). To turn them back on again you need to go deep into Outlook's options settings. On the **File** Backstage display menu click **Options**, then **Mail** and scroll down to **Message arrival**, and click to check the **Display a Desktop Alert** box.

Creating E-mail Signatures

It is often useful to supply your name, address and perhaps your e-mail address at the bottom of your outgoing e-mails. Outlook lets you do this with the **Signature** feature.

To create a signature, click **File** to display the Backstage menu, click **Options**, then **Mail**, scroll to **Compose messages**, and click the ⬚Signatures... button to open the dialogue box shown in Fig. 10.16.

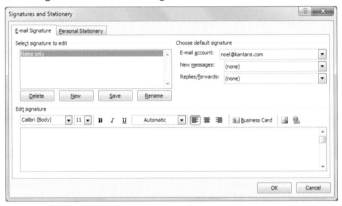

Fig. 10.16 The Signatures and Stationery Dialogue Box

If necessary, click the E-mail Signature tab and click the **New** button. Type a name for the signature (we typed 'Name only'), and then click **OK**. Next, you type the text that you want to include in the signature and format it with the style and formatting buttons. You can format your signature even if you use plain text as your message format. However, the formatting will only be visible to your mail recipients who use HTML or RTF message formats.

You can add an Electronic Business Card 📇, a picture 🖼 or hyperlinks 🔗 to your signature by clicking the appropriate buttons.

In the **Choose default signature** section, select the **E-mail account** which you always want to associate with the signature. If you only have one, this is automatic! In **New messages** select the signature you want to be automatically added to the end of each message. Select '(none)' if you don't want a signature used. After you finish creating the signature, click **OK**.

You could create several signatures with different content to be used depending on whether your e-mail is casual, formal or professional, and switch between them as required.

You can add or change the signature on a new message by clicking the **Signature** button in the **Include** group on the Ribbon and selecting from the drop-down list, as shown here in Fig. 10.17.

Fig. 10.17 Selecting a Signature

Junk E-mail Filter

The Junk E-mail Filter in Outlook 2010 is designed to catch junk messages or spam and send them to the **Junk E-mail** folder. It does this by examining each incoming message based on, when it was sent, its content and structure. The Filter is turned on by default, with Low protection, designed to catch the most obvious spam. You can make the filter more aggressive by changing the level of protection.

Messages sent to the **Junk E-mail** folder are converted to plain text and any links are disabled. You should check the messages in the Junk folder or you may lose important e-mails that have been incorrectly filtered out.

When the **Junk E-mail** folder is active the **Not Junk** option is added to the drop-down menu shown here in Fig. 10.18, so that you can retrieve such messages.

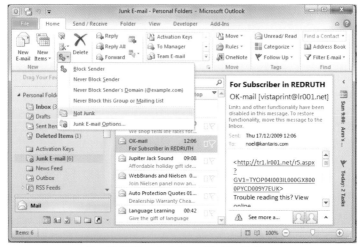

Fig. 10.18 The Junk E-mail Folder Options

Selecting the **Junk E-mail Options** from the above drop-down menu, displays the multi-tab Junk E-mail Options dialogue box shown in Fig. 10.19.

As you can see, there is a lot to choose from here. In the Options tab you can choose the level of protection, disable links, etc.

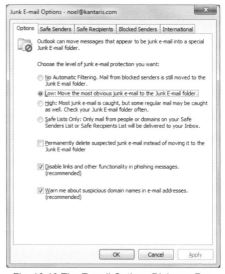

Fig. 10.19 The E-mail Options Dialogue Box

For the contents of the other tab screens, perhaps the Outlook Help system may be of use.

Safe Senders List – E-mail addresses and domain names in the Safe Senders List are never treated as junk e-mail, regardless of the content of the message. By default, all of the e-mail addresses in your Contacts are included in this list. E-mail addresses of people not listed in your Contacts but with whom you correspond are included in this list if you select the **Automatically add people I e-mail to the Safe Senders List** check box. (This check box is not selected by default.)

You can configure Outlook so that it accepts messages only from people in your Safe Senders List. This configuration gives you complete control over which messages are delivered to your **Inbox**.

Safe Recipients List – If you belong to a mailing list or a distribution list, you can add the list sender to the Safe Recipients List, so that messages sent from these e-mail addresses or domain names are never treated as junk, regardless of the content of the message.

Blocked Senders List – You can easily block messages from particular senders by adding their e-mail addresses or domain names to the Blocked Senders List. To do this, right-click the offending message in the Messages List and select the **Junk E-mail**, **Blocked Sender** option.

Fig. 10.20 Blocking a Sender

If you have existing lists of safe or blocked names and addresses, you can import them into Outlook.

International – To block unwanted e-mail messages that come from another country or region, you can add country/region codes to the Blocked Top-Level Domains List. To block unwanted e-mail messages in another language, add encodings to the Blocked Encodings List.

Deleting Junk Mail

To get rid of your junk mail, right-click the **Junk E-mail** Folder in the Navigation Pane and select the **Empty Folder** option.

To permanently delete individual messages from the **Junk E-mail** Folder without emptying it, select the message, and then press the **Delete** key on your keyboard.

Fig. 10.21 The Right-click Menu Options

You can also carry out some of these options from the Folder tab of the Ribbon, as shown below in Fig. 10.22 when the **Junk E-mail** folder is selected. The commands within the Clean Up group of the Folder tab change depending on which folder is selected.

Fig. 10.22 The Folder Tab of the Ribbon

Searching Folders

Selecting a folder and clicking the **New Search Folder** icon in Fig. 10.22 above, displays the dialogue box shown here. You can use this to create searches of your e-mail folders based on specific criteria, such as Unread mail, Mail flagged for follow up, Mail from people or lists.

Fig. 10.23 The New Search Folder Dialogue Box

Using E-mail Attachments

Attachments are files or Outlook items that can be sent as part of an e-mail message. Files can be drawings, documents, photos, or even sound and video files, and Outlook items can be messages, appointments, contacts, tasks, journal entries, notes, posted items and documents.

When you receive an e-mail in Outlook 2010 with an attachment it will have a paper clip icon 📎 in the Message List and the details of the attachment will appear in the attachment box below the Subject line, as shown in Fig. 10.24.

☑ Message | 🖼 027_Helathos south of Island.jpg (773 KB)

Fig. 10.24 The Attachment Box

For security reasons, Outlook blocks potentially unsafe attachment files with name extensions such as **.bat**, **.exe**, **.vbs** and **.js**, as they can contain viruses. Outlook does not block Microsoft Office document files, but make sure your anti-virus program has scanned them before you open them as they can contain macros that have the potential to spread viruses.

Previewing an Attachment

In Outlook 2010 you can quickly see what an attachment contains without opening it, by previewing it. Just clicking the attachment in the Reading Pane opens a preview as in Fig. 10.26 on the next page. Sometimes you might get the warning message displayed below in Fig. 10.25. To return to the message body, click the Message button.

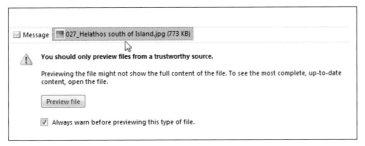

☑ Message | 🖼 027_Helathos south of Island.jpg (773 KB)

⚠ **You should only preview files from a trustworthy source.**

Previewing the file might not show the full content of the file. To see the most complete, up-to-date content, open the file.

Preview file

☑ Always warn before previewing this type of file.

Fig. 10.25 The Warning Message

To preview such a file click the **Preview file** button to open a screen similar to that shown below.

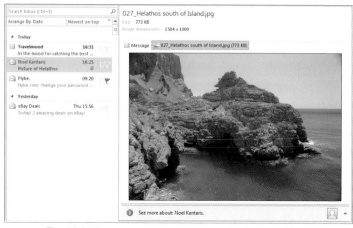

Fig. 10.26 Previewing an Attachment in the Reading Pane

To open an attachment you just double-click the attachment

button. There are several ways to save attachments, the easiest is probably to right-click the attachment button and on the shortcut menu (Fig. 10.27), click **Save As**. Choose a folder location, and then click **Save**.

Fig. 10.27 Shortcut Menu

To save multiple attachments click the **Save All Attachments** option on the menu.

Adding Attachments to your E-mail

If you want to include an attachment to your e-mail, simply click the **Message**, **Include**, **Attach File** (or the **Attach Item**) button on the Ribbon, shown in Fig. 10.28. Then select the file to attach in the Insert File dialogue box that opens.

Fig. 10.28 The Include Group

Printing your Messages

It was originally thought by some, that computers would lead to the paperless office. That has certainly not proved to be the case, as most people want to see the results printed on paper.

Outlook 2010 lets you print to paper either lists of details of all e-mail messages in a selected folder (details being: who sent the e-mail, its subject, when it was received and its size), or the actual contents of an e-mail.

To print a list of messages in a folder, select the folder, then use the **File**, **Print** command which displays the Print dialogue box shown in Fig. 10.29.

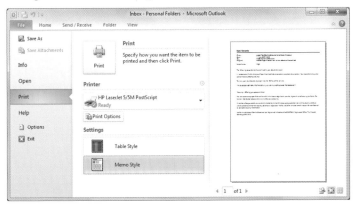

Fig. 10.29 Printing from Outlook 2010

Choosing the **Table Style** from the **Print style** options, allows you to use the **Page Setup** option to select the size and font of both the column headings of your lists and their rows. You can also choose the paper size, and whether to add headers or footers to the tables before committing to paper. Clicking the **Preview** button will show you what the print output will look like.

Selecting the **Memo Style** (the default) for the **Print style** options in the Print dialogue box, sends the contents of the selected message to the printer and prints out the actual contents of the message.

Make sure the correct printer, page range and number of copies you want are selected, then click the **OK** button.

You can also start the printing procedure by clicking the  **Print** button shown here. In this case the print job will be sent to the currently selected printer, using the current settings, so be careful when you use the **Print** button.

If the message has files attached to it and you want to print everything, then click the **Print attached files** box in the Print dialogue box to select it. However do note that attachments will print only to the default printer. For example, if you have printer A set as the default, and you open a message with an attachment and choose to print the e-mail to printer B, the message will be sent to printer B, but the attachment will go to printer A. So, if you have two printers, one black and white and one colour, and you want to print the attachments in colour make sure you assign the colour printer as the default.

To do this with Windows 7, click the Windows **Start** button (at the left end of the Taskbar) and click **Devices and Printers** to open the folder shown in Fig. 10.30 below.

Fig. 10.30 The Windows Devices and Printers Folder

Here, several printer drivers have been installed and the HP LaserJet 5M is set as the default printer, with a tick ✅ in its icon. To change this, right-click on another printer in the list, and select **Set as default Printer** from the context menu.

Using RSS Feeds

 With Outlook 2010, you can now read and manage your blogs and RSS Feeds from within the application, at the same time as handling your e-mail and calendar.

RSS stands for 'Really Simple Syndication'. They are also called 'Feeds' and are just Web pages, designed to be read by computers rather than people. RSS is a way for publishers of online news agencies and magazines to make news, blogs, and other content freely available to subscribers. You find what you want, subscribe to it, and then every time the author updates the content or writes something new, it is delivered straight to Outlook on your desk. Feeds offer an easy way to keep up to date with what you are interested in.

The usual way to find a new RSS Feed is to look on your favourite Web sites and if they offer this feature, you will see the 🔊 icon in colour. Clicking such an icon will open a Feed page. If you like it, look for the link that lets you 'subscribe' and click it, as shown in Fig. 10.31.

Fig. 10.31 Subscribing to a Feed Using Explorer

Fig. 10.32 The Subscribe to a Feed
Dialogue Box

This opens the Subscribe to this Feed dialogue box, shown in Fig. 10.32. Clicking the **Subscribe** button completes the procedure. Next, you need to synchronise Outlook 2010 with the **Common Feeds List in Windows**, provided you are using Internet Explorer 7 or 8.

Windows allows Outlook 2010 to share RSS Feeds via the **Common Feeds List in Windows**, which is a common location for RSS Feeds, with Internet Explorer 7 or 8. Deleting an RSS Feed from the common location, removes it from all programs that access it. However, deleting an RSS Feed in Outlook 2010, does not remove it from other participating programs, such as Internet Explorer.

To synchronise an RSS Feed to Outlook 2010 for the first time, click the **File** command button on the Ribbon, then click **Options**, followed by **Advanced**. In the displayed screen, scroll to RSS Feeds, and click the **Synchronize RSS Feeds to the Common Feed List (CFL) in Windows** check box to select it, then click **OK**.

Next time you start Outlook, expanding the Navigation Pane displays the **RSS Feeds** 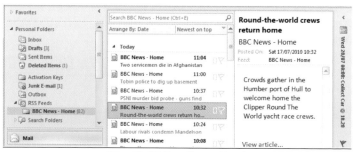 folder with a sub-folder containing the **BBC News – Home** feed we subscribed to, and displaying for us 82 feeds, as shown in Fig. 10.33.

Fig. 10.33 Reading a Feed

When you select an RSS Feed, its downloaded contents are displayed, as shown above. Outlook 2010 checks the RSS publisher's server for new and updated items regularly.

To remove the RSS Feeds facility from Outlook, simply click the **File** button, then **Options**, **Advanced**, and in the displayed screen, click the **Synchronize RSS Feeds to the Common Feed List (CFL) in Windows** check box to deselect it, then click **OK**. To remove an RSS Feeds sub-folder, select it and press the **Del** keyboard key.

11

Other Outlook 2010 Features

Using the Calendar

The Calendar is the diary and scheduling view of Outlook 2010 in which you can, create and manage appointments, meetings and events. Before we start entering information in our Calendar, we will take a look at its opening screen. There are several ways to open the Calendar. Clicking the **Calendar** button in the Navigation Pane (pointed to below), or use the **Ctrl+2** keyboard shortcut. Both open the Calendar shown in Fig. 11.1 below. Clicking a date on the Date Navigator, opens a Day view of Calendar.

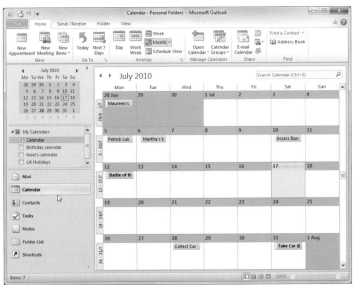

Fig. 11.1 The Outlook Calendar in Month View

Here we have the Navigation Pane open, which includes the Date Navigator and My Calendars. You can close or minimise these to give more room for the Calendar itself.

You use the buttons on the Ribbon at the top of the Calendar window (in the **Arrange** group) to change your Calendar view, or the other buttons mentioned below to navigate through your Calendar and to show or hide other Calendars as follows:

Click on **Day**, **Work**, **Week**, or **Month** to quickly switch views.

You can use the Date Navigator at the top of the Navigation pane to open the Calendar on a specific day. The arrow buttons at the top move forward or backward one month.

The **Back** and **Forward** buttons next to the date at the top left of the Calendar area, allow you to easily move through your calendar.

My Calendars pane in the Navigation pane, lets you see or hide additional Calendars, if you created or downloaded them, such as Birthday calendar, or UK Holidays.

The **Views** buttons on the Status bar shown in Fig. 11.2 also lets you quickly change your view of the Calendar.

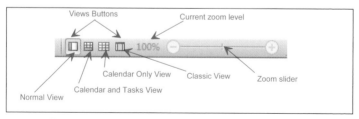

Fig. 11.2 The Views and Zoom Buttons on the Task Bar

Some Definitions

Before you start scheduling an appointment, meeting or event, it is necessary to look at some Calendar definitions:

- An appointment does not involve other colleagues or resources, and can be recurring, that is it can be repeated on a regular basis.

- A meeting is an appointment that involves other people and possibly resources, and can also be recurring.

- An event is an activity that lasts one day or more, such as attendance at an exhibition or conference. An annual event occurs yearly on a specific date. Events and annual events do not occupy blocks of time in your Calendar; instead, they appear as a banner below the current day heading.

- A task is an activity that involves only you, and that doesn't need a scheduled time.

Entering Appointments

As an example we will now create a recurring appointment to, say, meet Section Managers, that takes place on the third Wednesday every month starting at 10:00 a.m. on 21 July and lasts for 2 hours.

To do so, click the 21 July on the Date Navigator at the top of the Navigation Pane, or navigate in the Calendar to it,

Fig. 11.3 Setting the Start Time

move the cursor to 10:00 a.m., and click to start adding a new appointment, as shown in Fig. 11.3. Type 'Managers' meeting' and double-click the entry to open the Appointment window displayed in Fig. 11.4 on the next page in which you can type 'My Office' in the **Location** box, set the **End time** to 12.00, and maybe enter some text in the main body with a little more detail.

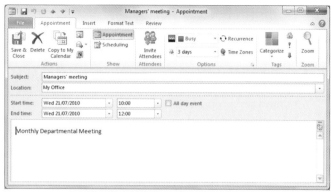

Fig. 11.4 Entering a New Appointment

Next, press the **Recurrence** 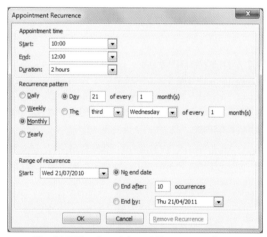 button on the Ribbon to open the Appointment Recurrence dialogue box shown in Fig. 11.5 below.

Fig. 11.5 The Appointment Recurrence Box

Click the **Monthly** radio button, select the **Recurrence pattern** offered of the third Wednesday every month as shown, and click **OK**. Finally, click the **Save and Close** button shown here and located in the **Actions** group on the Ribbon of the Appointment window.

Fig. 11.6 New Appointment and Drop-down Menu

The Calendar entry now shows the new appointment, including location of meeting, together with the **Recurring** symbol 🔄, and the time span which has a blue background.

If you want to make any changes to the newly created appointment just right-click in it to open the menu shown in Fig. 11.6. You can use the options on this drop-down menu to print, edit, or delete the appointment. Choosing the **Open** option, displays the Open Recurring Appointment dialogue box where you can select to open this occurrence only or the whole series, so that changes can be applied appropriately.

Appointments also show on the To-Do Bar on the right of the screen when in **Classic** view, as long as there is room for them. This depends on how many you have set up. We prefer to set up Calendar in the Classic view, which is also the default view of all other Outlook views (Mail, Contacts, Tasks and Notes). From all these views you can keep a check on your appointments.

By default you will get a reminder window opening on top of everything else on the screen 15 minutes before the appointment start time. If this is not long enough, you can set the reminder time to up to 2 weeks in advance in the **Options** group on the Ribbon of the Appointment window.

Entering Events

An event is an activity that lasts all day long and is entered into the Calendar in the same way as an appointment. Birthdays and holidays are events. Let us now assume that your Mother's birthday is on the 5th of August. To enter this click the 5th August on the Date Navigator at the top of the Classic view bar and double-click somewhere on that day's calendar page. This opens the Appointment window. Type 'Mother's Birthday' in the **Subject** box and click the **All day event** check box, pointed to in Fig. 11.7 on the next page.

Fig. 11.7 Entering a New Event

The window now changes to an Event window, as shown above. Next, click the **Recurrence** button on the Ribbon to open the Appointment Recurrence dialogue box shown previously in Fig. 11.5. Click the **Yearly** radio button, click **OK** and finally, click the **Save and Close** button to create the event, as shown in Classic view in Fig. 11.8 below.

Fig. 11.8 The New Event shown in the Calendar Window

That's all there is to it, you should never miss your important dates again, but you must make time to enter them in Calendar in the first place. Go on; try it!

Printing Information

Information held in a diary can be printed on paper. Simply use the **File, Print** command to open the Print dialogue box in Fig. 11.9 on the facing page.

In the Printer **Name** box, at the top of the dialogue box, click the down arrow to select from one of the installed printers on your system. Next, choose an appropriate item from the **Print style** list, then use the **Print Options** button, and click the **Page Setup** button to see the format, page size and header/footer options of the selected print style.

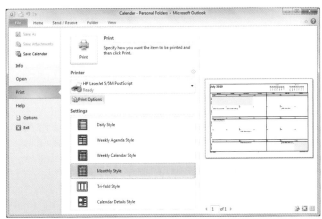

Fig. 11.9 The Calendar Print Dialogue Box

In Fig. 11.10 below, we show the Page Setup dialogue box with the Header/Footer tab selected. Note the five icon buttons pointed to below the Footer text boxes. These can be used to insert page number, total number of pages, date, time and user's name respectively, in both headers and footers. To do so, simply place the insertion cursor on one of the text boxes, then click the appropriate button.

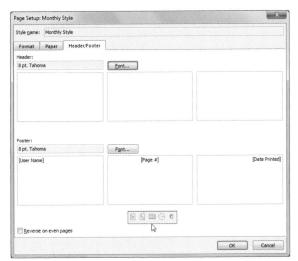

Fig. 11.10 Inserting a Footer in the Page Setup Dialogue Box

In the above footer set-up, we have inserted the user's name in the left panel of the footer, the page number in the middle panel, and the date printed in the right panel. If you decide to show such information on your printout, it is entirely up to you where you choose to insert it. You can also change the font type and font size of the information appearing on a header or footer.

If you want to change the font type and font size of the text appearing on the actual body of your printout, click the Format tab of the above dialogue box, and make appropriate selections under the displayed **Font** section. Pressing the **OK** button on the Page Setup dialogue box returns you to the Print dialogue box. However, before committing anything to paper, click the **Preview** button on the Print dialogue box and save a few trees!

Planning a Meeting

Suppose we decide to invite other people into the meeting with the Managers on 18th August. First, locate the date of the meeting on the Calendar display and double-click the entry in question. In the displayed 'Recurring Item' box, click the **Open this occurrence** radio button to display the Recurring Appointment window.

Next, click the **Scheduling** button to change to a Recurring Meeting window as shown in Fig. 11.11 on the next page. Here we just typed the names of two colleagues we would like to be present at the meeting. If you had a Contacts list (see next section), you could also select people from it to attend this meeting by simply clicking the **Add Others** button, then clicking the **Add from Address Book** option, and selecting from the displayed list.

From here, you can organise meetings and send e-mail requests to participants and then track the status of their response provided, of course, you are either connected to a local network or know their e-mail address. You can even give other Outlook users permissions to view your diary and to plan meetings with you at times when you are not so busy, but still be able to maintain private information in your diary.

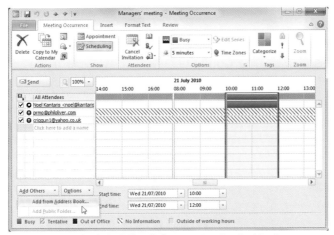

Fig. 11.11 Scheduling Colleagues to attend a Meeting

Please Note:
We have only been able to cover the Outlook Calendar very briefly. To get more information on this very useful feature we suggest you browse the Calendar and Scheduling section of Outlook 2010's Help system.

As well as the Calendar, the other view options on the Navigation Pane of Outlook 2010 contain all the elements needed to give you a very effective time-management tool.

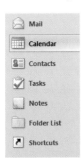

Fig. 11.12
Buttons in the
Navigation Pane

These elements are most quickly accessed, as we have already seen, by clicking the buttons located at the bottom of the Navigation Pane, shown here in Fig. 11.12. You can also use the keyboard shortcuts shown here in Fig. 11.13.

TO DO THIS	PRESS
Switch to Mail.	CTRL+1
Switch to Calendar.	CTRL+2
Switch to Contacts.	CTRL+3
Switch to Tasks.	CTRL+4
Switch to Notes.	CTRL+5
Switch to Folder List	CTRL+6
Switch to Shortcuts.	CTRL+7

Fig. 11.13 Keyboard
Shortcuts

Contacts

In Outlook your 'Contacts' are the people you send the most messages to. The **Contacts** view displays your contacts in several ways, such as business cards or various list views. You can change the way information is displayed by clicking one of the **Change View** list formats, as shown below. What is shown here is a 'somewhat edited' version of part of our Business Cards view – you have the choice of three other types of views.

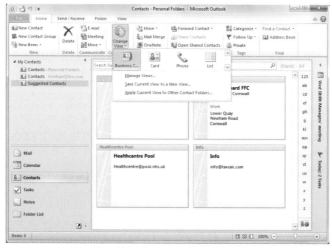

Fig. 11.14 Business Cards View

To add a new contact, click the **New Contact** button, shown here, or to edit an existing entry, double-click on the contact name. Either action displays the Contact window, shown in Fig. 11.15 on the facing page, in which you type relevant information. We have only ever bothered to type details in the General section, as shown, but if you want, you can include someone's whole history by filling in the other sections. You can even add a photograph for each of your contacts by double-clicking the button pointed to in Fig. 11.15 and browsing to the folder that holds them. When you have finished click the **Save and Close** button to file your new contact's details away.

Fig. 11.15 Details of a Fictitious Contact

Contact lists can be saved under different group names, so that you could have one list for your personal friends, and another for your business contacts.

The task of filling in such detailed information about an individual might be daunting at first, but if you persevere, you will find it very useful later. You can then use the controls in the **Communicate** group (shown above) to instantly make contact in various ways. For example, you only have to left-click on the **Web Page** button in the **More** command drop-down menu (shown open in Fig. 11.15 above), to be automatically connected to a contact's Web page. Clicking the **Call** button instead, opens the AutoDialer and connects to your contact by phone, as long as you are set up to do this!

Try clicking the **Map It** button. This opens a **bing Maps** Web page and locates the contact's address on it. This only works though, provided you have entered the address in the **Address** box at the bottom of the Contact screen and included the Postcode. Try it with a real address, it works really well.

The Address Book

The Name, Display Name and E-mail Address of all your

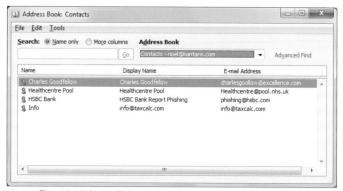

Outlook Contacts are added to the default Address Book. As e-mail addresses are often quite complicated and not at all easy to remember this can be a very useful feature. To open it you can click the **Home**, **Find**, **Address Book** button on the Outlook 2010 Ribbon. Fig. 11.16 below shows part of one of ours.

Fig. 11.16 Some Extracts from the Contacts Address Book

Outlook allows you to access e-mail addresses from either the Address Book/Contacts list or the Global Address Book list. However, the latter requires you to be using a Microsoft Exchange Server e-mail account and its list contains the names and e-mail addresses of everyone in your organisation. The Microsoft Exchange Server administrator is the only person that can create and maintain this address book.

Once in the Address Book, you can edit an entry by double-clicking it to open the Contact window seen before in Fig. 11.15. If you want, you can manually add a new person's full details with the **File**, **New Entry** menu command and select **New Contact** in the displayed New Entry dialogue box. Clicking the **OK** button, again opens the Contact window of Fig. 11.15. The **File**, **New Message** menu command starts a new message to the selected contact.

To send a new message to anyone listed in your Address Book/Contacts list, open a New Message window and click on any of the **To:** or **Cc:** icons shown here on the left.

In the Select Names box which is opened (Fig. 11.17), you can select a person's name and click either the **To->** button to place it in the **To** field of your message, the **Cc->** button to place it in the **Cc** field, or the **Bcc->**button to place it in the **Bcc** field.

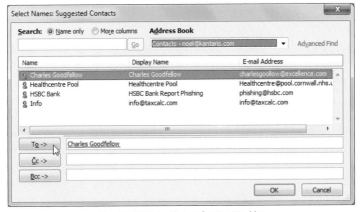

Fig. 11.17 Selecting a Contact to Use

Note: Cc is an abbreviation for carbon copy. If you add a recipient's name to this box in a message, a copy of the message is sent to that recipient, and the recipient's name is visible to other recipients of the message.

Bcc is an abbreviation for blind carbon copy. If you add a recipient's name to this box in a message, a copy of the message is sent to that recipient, and the recipient's name is not visible to other recipients of the message. The **Bcc** field becomes visible in a New Outlook message when you add recipients to the corresponding field in Fig. 11.17.

Tasks

A 'task' is an item that you create in Outlook to track until it is completed. A 'to-do' item is an Outlook item, like a task, an e-mail message, or a contact, that has been flagged for follow-up. By default, all tasks are flagged for follow-up when they are created, even if they have no start date or due date. Therefore, whenever you create a task, or flag an e-mail message or a contact, a to-do item is created automatically. Both tasks and to-do items appear in Tasks, as shown below in the To-Do Bar and in the Task List in all the other Outlook activities (Mail, Calendar, Contacts and Notes)..

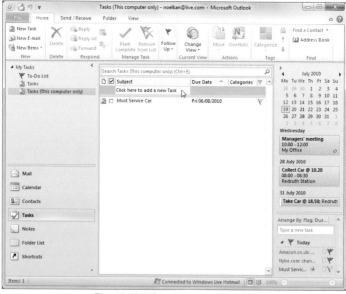

Fig. 11.18 A Simple To-Do Task List

The Tasks view, shown in Fig. 11.18, is opened by clicking the **Tasks** button at the middle of the Navigation Pane, then selecting one of the options from the **My Tasks** list. Here we chose the **Tasks (This computer only)** option.

To create a new task, either click the **Home**, **New Task** button on the Ribbon, or double-click the box pointed to above. Either of these opens the window in Fig. 11.19.

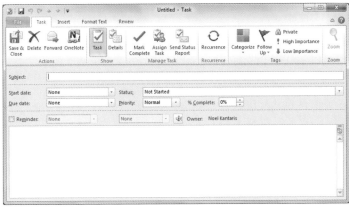

Fig. 11.19 Creating a New Task in the Task Window

If you have the To-Do Bar open you can enter a task in its **Type a new task** text box from any view in Outlook. Also, in Tasks view you click and type in the **Click here to add a new Task** text box pointed to in Fig. 11.18.

We find we use the To-Do Bar most often to add and update tasks, and to mark them as complete.

Tasks can be assigned to other people within your organisation, and can help you keep track of progress on

work that other people do for you or in co-operation with you. To assign a task, you first create it, and then click the **Assign Task** button shown here, to send it as a task request to someone.

To find out more about Tasks we suggest you use the Outlook Help system and search for 'tasks'. Look through the various topics listed in the Help window and work through all of them. Using Help in this way, you will quickly learn how to sort and give priority to tasks, track their progress, enter recurring tasks, assign tasks to others and keep complex task lists organised. Good luck.

Notes

If you are the type that sticks notes all over your desk to remind you of things, you will be happy to know that Outlook lets you create electronic 'sticky' notes. They remain on the Desktop until you close them or you close Outlook, but remain in Notes until you delete them.

When you start the Notes activity, and you want to create a new note, click the **New Note** button on the Ribbon. The result for two such notes, is shown in Fig. 11.20.

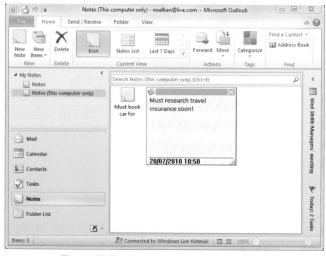

Fig. 11.20 The Notes View with an Open Note

To create a new note from any other Outlook activity use the **Ctrl+Shift+N** keyboard shortcut.

You can type whatever text you want in the note, and edit it at any time. Changes are saved automatically. You can also drag a note on the desktop.

To close the note displayed on the desktop, right-click it and click **Delete** from the drop-down menu. The note is removed from the desktop, but remains in Notes. To delete a note from Notes, select it and click the **Delete** icon on the Ribbon.

Journal

In Outlook's Journal you can select to automatically record actions relating to specified contacts and to place the actions in a Timeline view. In addition to tracking Outlook items, such as e-mail, or other Office documents, such as Word or Excel files, you can keep a record of any interaction you want to remember, such as a telephone conversation or a letter you mailed or received.

You could usefully use Journal to record the dates and times of your interactions with contacts, such as tracking hours spent on a particular account. If you want to create a list of all the items related to a contact, use activity tracking instead, to link the items to that contact.

To start Journal, click the **Folder List** button on the Navigation pane, which displays the **Journal** button under the **Personal Folders**, then click the **Journal** button, to display the screen in Fig. 11.21.

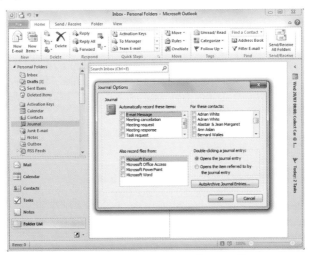

Fig. 11.21 The Journal Options Dialogue Box

To find out how to use the various functions appearing on a Journal list, use the Office Help system and search for 'Journal'.

Backing Up Outlook Data

Unless you are using a Microsoft Exchange account or an HTTP account, such as Windows Live Mail, all of your Outlook data will be saved in the Personal Folders file (**Outlook.pst**). This file contains all of your Outlook folders, including the Inbox, Calendar and Contacts. By default you will have a single **.pst** file (usually called Personal Folders in your Folder List).

To back up your **.pst** file, use the method discussed in Chapter 9 under **Importing Data into Outlook** (page 184). In particular, use the **File** button, then select the **Open** command on the Backstage screen and click the **Import** option. This opens the Import and Export Wizard dialogue box (see Fig. 9.12 on page 185). At the top of the screen you see **Export to a file** entry. Select this option and in the Export to a File dialogue box, select the **Outlook Data File (.pst)** entry, then select each folder you want to back up, and follow the screen instructions of the Wizard.

Microsoft suggests that if you cannot open the **.pst** file, to use their Inbox repair toolkit first. The file you need to run is called **Scabpst.exe** and is located in the C:\Program Files\Microsoft Office\Office14 folder. However, Outlook must be closed before you double-click this file. Then, supply the drive where your **.pst** file is located, and follow the instructions on screen.

* * *

In the last three chapters, we have tried to cover sufficient information on Outlook 2010, so that you can get to grips with the program and get on with the job of sending and receiving e-mail effectively, this being one of the most used activities on the Internet.

Outlook has more features, too numerous to discuss in the space allocated here. What we have tried to do, is give you enough basic information so that you can have the confidence to explore the rest of Outlook's capabilities by yourself. Have fun!

Index